Staying Married

MARGARET FRINGS KEYES

Staying Married

LES FEMMES
MILLBRAE, CALIFORNIA

301,42
K437⊿
1975

Copyright © 1975 by Celestial Arts
231 Adrian Road, Millbrae, California 94030

First printing: November 1975
Made in the United States of America

   2 3 4 5 6 7 8 – 80 79 78 77 76

Library of Congress Cataloging in Publication Data

Keyes, Margaret Frings, 1929-
    Staying married.

    1. Marriage. 2. Problem family. 3. Interpersonal
relations. I. Title.
HQ734.K44   301.42   75-9443
ISBN 0-89087-986-9 cloth
ISBN 0-89087-902-8 paper

Contents

Introduction

Chapter I
The Value of Marital Crisis   1

Chapter II
The Clash of Expectations — The Crisis Exposed   11

Chapter III
How Did We Get to This Point?   30

Chapter IV
Marital Problem Analysis   50

Chapter V
Problem Solving   75

Chapter VI
What's Right with Marriage   94

Chapter VII
Crisis and Reconnecting: Therapy of a Marriage   107

Chapter VIII
The Future of Marriage   133

Appendix   141

Bibliography   142

Types of Marital Therapists   149

Index   156

Introduction

A higher proportion of people enter marriage today than a hundred years ago. For all the interest in communes and lifestyles with "alternatives to marriage," the research evidence is that one man in relationship to one woman with some bond of commitment between them is not only the most highly desired way of being together but also works best, even in the communes.

Still, the statistics are staggering. There was one divorce for every 1,234 marriages a hundred years ago. At the turn of the century it was up to one for every 500 marriages, then one per 12 in 1920, one per every 6 in 1940 and 1 per 3 today. Eighty percent of those who divorce remarry and these marriages tend to last. The birthrate is down but increasing numbers of children are being raised in either one-parent families or with a stepparent. These facts reflect but also can not help but influence attitudes toward marriage. It seems paradoxical that in a time when individuals aspire to greater awareness, freedom and their own personal growth, so many have difficulty finding it in marriage, which research indicates is one of the greatest bulwarks for mental health. What's happening?

Contemporary marriage has great potential in it and resources available to it. More than ever, couples are free to focus on their relationship. Being married and working at it is a basic goal for most people. There has been a knowledge explosion in the last quarter century in the behavioral sciences which offers enormous help in facilitating personal and marital growth. There is much greater awareness of the need for intimacy and the communication of deep interpersonal love between partners. Marriage and family education and counseling have become widely available but many are unable to tap this potential and need more help than they are getting or utilizing.

There are many difficulties. While people are freer to work at relationships, they experience difficulty in communicating. There is more help available in the community but less from extended family members who offer perspective from their own experience and also know a lot about other family members and their ways. There is more mobility and opportunity for families today but also less stability and security. There are more alternatives and options but more decision making pressure. More education but more awareness of loss of simplicity in living. More autonomy among family members but fewer home experiences of natural emotions. The sexual revolution has liberated many women but causes real value confusion for most. In setting high goals of companionship, intimacy and acceptance, the almost inevitable experiences of isolation and rejection are devastating.

The fact that second marriages tend to last and that people tend to choose partners much like the ones they chose the first time suggests that there has been some process of learning in the second relationship and some modification of expectations or of the processes in marriage.

This book takes the point of view that crises are an important element within marriage. They do not have to end in divorce or in a deadly war of endurance. They are growth points.

In times of crisis, both partners are off balance and open to learning some difficult facts — realities about their relationship that do not jibe with either person's expectations or wishes. If the tendency to escalate the war and the defensive collecting of ammunition can be contained, a crisis can be an extremely important time of growth for both partners personally. Resources are mobilized and strengths are identified. But also, life has some very dark aspects to it. Pain in facing one's limitations and one's losses recurs for every man, for every woman. Positive and negative feelings go together. These core feelings in the marital relationship have to be shared, accepted and responded to. Each person experiences these deep feelings as frighteningly tender, so in order to avoid hurt, easily, strongly and commonly defends them.

Partners have to learn to overcome their own and each other's defenses which block off their deeper feeling for one another. It is important to recognize the defenses for what they are. The ones with words include both excessive talking and silence, speaking in a monotone, using abstract words or long prefaces that never get to the point, the games of belittling, being overly critical, changing the subject, playing dumb. The nonverbal defenses include nervous laughter, the smile when one is really hurt or angry, avoiding eye contact, keeping a poker face, suppressing anger, pretending sleep, over-involvement outside the family or with the children, absorption in TV, pretending not to hear, being mechanical in showing affection, etc. Psychological defenses include denial that there is a problem, withdrawal, refusal to talk about it, taking it out on someone else or something else, seeing others as having the problems that really belong to oneself, rationalizing one's position, accepting peace at any price. In coping with one's reactions to these defenses it is hard to realize that they are hiding some very different and quite vulnerable feelings in the other partner. It takes personal risk to find this out.

Motivation to change the marriage relationship comes

from two sources—discomfort and hope. The situation has to be really experienced as a bad scene, thoroughly, totally and completely unacceptable. Paradoxically, it is sometimes only when one or both partners are for the first time considering divorce that a sufficient degree of discomfort has been reached that energy for change becomes available. Hope, however, is equally necessary. The experience and knowledge of the other partner's caring in the past is an important element, even when this does not seem to be a current reality. The experience of former problems and crises that have been worked through also builds hope and develops trust in the value of crises and the process of resolution. Knowledge of the experiences of other people, relatives and friends who have worked at their differences to form a richer relationship also helps. But these may be missing or insufficiently known. Hope can be gained from the knowledge that there are resources for help in counseling— family service agencies, ministers and priests, clinical social workers, psychologists, psychiatrists as well as group movements for the enrichment of marriage and family life education courses.

This book is also addressed to hope. This book is for you if you are in a marriage you value but are finding difficult. It will help you identify how you block feelings and build toward crisis in the clash of your expectations. You will link these expectations with various subpersonalities within you and your partner to learn why they have such violent antipathy and where and how they might be better joined. You will learn some specific methods to understand the development of your relationship with its particular kinks.

Many of the difficulties experienced in marriage, however, are not basically rooted in conditioning, inabilities or lack of insight. They are linked to problems within our society. You will look at major marital problem areas—money, power, sex and affection, children and the use of alcohol in this light. You will acquire some thorough training in modern communication theory and constructive fighting which allows you to drop the "right-wrong" games and allows both of you to win. You'll learn something of different personality types and the kind of effort that opposites have to make to understand one another. You'll learn something of the strengths and resources available in marriage and how to identify your own. And, if you want additional help, there is an indepth look at what the process of marriage therapy can involve for a marital relationship and for the individual person. Finally there are suggestions on further resources and how to evaluate them.

Not all marriage crises can be resolved so the marriage continues. And in the marriages which do continue, what has been broken can never be restored to its original condition. There is always evidence of the changes which have been experienced but there is also an invariably more interesting, more "human" character to such marriages and to the people who constitute them. It is for more such marriages that this book is written.

DEDICATION

For Vincent and for Bill
and for the couples whose lives we touch and who touch ours

ACKNOWLEDGEMENTS

Much of the content of this book evolved in the therapy groups for couples which I have led over the years with William M. Lamers, Jr., M.D. I am indebted to him and to his wife, Clara Lamers, for their critical reading of the initial draft and to Jerry Houston for her reading of the final manuscript.

I am grateful to my husband, Vincent Keyes, for his patience, to my editor, George Young, for his persistence and to my clients for their permission to use, with disguised names, examples from their life experiences.

Chapter I

The Value of Marital Crisis

The Chinese character for crisis indicates two things—danger and change. In time of crisis things are off balance. Crisis is a time when "the last straw," added to what has gone before, can bring down a whole structure. It is also a time when a relatively small amount of energy properly applied can shift the structure in a new direction and the fall-out can lead to greater stability.

We are living in a time when marriage is under heavy pressure—crisis, danger and anxiety exist. Where such situations exist, the possibility of a positive shift *also* exists to bring renewal and rebirth to the relationship. Crisis need not signal the end of relationship. It can be a call for a deeper, more honest reality. Even in a growing or "good" relationship, marriage in some sense is one crisis after another. In any marriage our self-centered patterns of existence are challenged. Even in a marriage that has reached a stage near dissolution, the possibility of renewal exists. The possibility may be smothered under mountains of righteous rage, hurt, or perhaps sheer boredom, but if you want to look and know where, the possibility can grow.

1

For instance, Polly and Steve, a young couple were on the brink of divorce. Polly had already moved out and was living with another man, but agreed to come to therapy because Steve was depressed and also showing a fury she had not seen before. Polly had married Steve because she admired his talent and vision and shared his idealism. For four years they were the "perfect married couple." Polly's leaving came as a complete shock to Steve. He couldn't understand it. All Polly would say was that everything was so perfect, she somehow didn't feel alive. As they worked in therapy, it became clear that Polly had lost touch with her own creativity, judging it to be so much less than Steve's. She had no separate sphere where his talents did not overshadow her own. He was understanding and supportive and *never* got angry. They never fought but she felt some wild animal urge in her struggling to be free. Her involvement with another man she recognized, was a frantic attempt to break through the rigid patterns of their life together.

Oddly enough, the direction to follow in crisis is the one that initially you feel you would do almost anything to deny and avoid — down into the pain and darkness of really facing and experiencing the death of old expectations. "This isn't what I thought it would be." "I feel hurt, deprived, numb with an unfilled hunger." Whatever the feelings are, it is difficult to own them and to experience just how bad they feel but that *is* the essential beginning.

Awareness comes from staying with the pain. The death of old expectations and points of view can open the possibility of rebirth of a relationship.

Steve lost the image he had of Polly as a perfect and faithful wife and he was forced to recognize his own anger. In doing so, he had to look more closely at what he was doing with his anger in other situations and how in denying anger he also lost passion and power. As he began to reconnect with this, Polly again was drawn to him, this time as to a more complete man. For herself, she had recognized that she had to take responsibility for her separate talents, without discounting them as less than Steve's.

Unfortunately, two other choices often seem to offer an easier out than staying with the pain:

1. *You can deny there is a crisis.* You repress your feeling response and regress to earlier solutions or substitute satisfactions—eat more, work harder, distract yourself with shopping, bridge, TV, church, club activities, or even sleep.
2. *You flee from fully experiencing your feelings.* You do not confront the strength and depth of your anger or possibly the humiliation of loss of face or hurt. The choice of divorce can be made in order to avoid the pain of self-confrontation and confrontation with partner rather than as the result of the painful relationship.

Marital crisis forces you to know yourself, your limitations and some aspects you'd prefer not to see. It can also, however, develop your strength and bring out new parts of your person with a greater sense of wholeness.

Jane, at sixty-three, clung to her second marriage as the only security she knew. But she recognized that things could not continue as they had been. Even public aid was better than the lack of self-respect she felt staying with an impossible relationship. She found ways she could become self-sufficient. When her brother lent her the money to develop a small catering service, her natural vivacity returned and she developed a sense of self-sufficiency which enabled her to continue to work at the relationship problems.

The initial step in weathering a crisis is to find ways to express feelings about the discomfort in each partner and the realities they represent.

If the crisis is severe, professional help can be invaluable. An objective third person—a minister, a social worker in a family agency, a psychologist, psychiatrist, or marriage counselor can help. By listening to your feelings, such a person can often enable you to hear more of the complexity of these feelings. You can become clearer about your options—

what needs to change and what to do next. The professional's knowledge of normal human behavior helps you regain perspective. The professional's knowledge of community resources can also be useful for specific difficulties, e.g. alcohol and financial or legal issues. A marriage therapy group gives you a perspective that no other approach can match. You can see the essence of another couple in conflict so much more clearly than your own. You can begin to identify the common elements, the many disguises of feeling.

Most marital crises are the kind that develop gradually. You hardly notice the difficult feelings. They seem so familiar. *Think about it now, right this minute.* What is the unpleasant feeling that you know best, the one you have most often—hurt, anger, self-pity, depression, hopelessness, or whatever. There is a good chance that it is a cover feeling for something else. Often without your awareness you find it easier to feel one kind of feeling rather than another—hurt rather than anger, rage rather than fear, or sometimes confusion rather than any feeling at all. The difficulty comes when you act on any of these "easier" feelings rather than checking out all that you are feeling.

For instance, it may be easier for you to feel angry than hurt if you grew up in a family where toughness worked and where if you showed tears, you were dismissed as a crybaby. So now your temptation is to act on the anger, slam out of the house, threaten divorce, react to get out and avoid the difficult feeling of your hurt. Or maybe you close in with icy or heated words, pointing out the defects of character, the numerous faults and failures of the other. Again you are smokescreening, avoiding either one of you becoming aware of your own hurt.

People often get angry when their feelings are hurt. If you allow your anger to grow without expressing it, you can begin to feel guilt about the anger. Too much guilt leads to feelings of worthlessness and depression. Unless the hurt is expressed also, the issue is still not resolved.

For example, Pete, a charming gregarious man, felt increasingly at odds with his wife, Liz. Everyone else appreciated his talent and personality but Liz was invariably sarcastic and angry with him after a party, then silent and glum. It simply did not occur to him that she could be angry with him because he was charming and amusing to strangers and yet found nothing to say to her when they were alone.

This type of feeling reaction comes from only part of you. It is almost as if you had an inner group of sub-selves and your most familiar difficult feeling comes from the part of you that learned to hide the real feeling. It did not pay in an earlier life situation to show it. This cover feeling at least gets some attention and releases some of your discomfort. The problem is that it does not lead to any real meeting between you and your partner now because it is essentially beside the point. You find yourself constantly in conflict, constantly *proving* you are right even though it does not make you feel good.

When things are not working right, most of us tend to look for fault and place responsibility. Our cause-effect mentality vastly over-simplifies. However, when our self-esteem is threatened, it seems so obvious that the other is at fault—surely we would not do this to ourselves!

Conflicts in themselves are not so important. There are differences in taste—Montovani vs. Mozart, antique vs. modern, conservative vs. liberal. It is *how conflicts are used* that is important. Conflicts are the language of anger. Conflicts are used as ammunition. For example, if you refuse to eat your wife's special French cooking because you are into health foods or if you always come late or you are "not hungry" at mealtime, you are not fighting over food. Food is an excuse, a means for paying her back with anger at something not so easily seen.

Maybe you love sports or card games. Maybe your partner loathes them and resists every effort to get involved. He may worry that he won't do well and does not want to be judged a failure. Games are not the problem. Your partner goes to bed at 9; you watch the late show. You are always ready for a party; your partner is always too tired. Each of you somehow manages to disappoint the other. Something deeper is signaling for attention.

What I am proposing is that you stop acting from your customary feeling, which is probably only the surface one anyway. Try to uncover the emotion that is using the conflict as a means of expressing itself. Let the under feelings emerge, the deeper hidden feelings. Initially this is difficult. You probably resist clarifying the ambiguity of your situation. Familiarity is a veil. It hides the problems which need to be worked with under a blanket of tacit agreements not to disturb the existing order. Better this than the dreaded possibility of having the whole thing come apart. You need to take time and to risk breaking the patterns of your life together if you want to grow.

"Well, I'm willing but she won't." "He doesn't go for all this analysis and feeling talk." O.K. if he or she joins you initially or later matters not too much. Only you have access to the place for you to begin — *exploring your own perceptions of you.* You must explore all of what you feel, what you know has gone wrong, or does not hang together. *You* must find the basic elements, the values in marriage which for you are essential. Values deal with your style of behaving and with the goals of your existence that you consider worth working toward. For instance, you might value being consistent, being productive, having a sense of humor. Communicating, openly, all that you feel about your partner may not be one of your values. Your marital goal values may involve raising your children to the age of 18, when you believe they should become self-sufficient, or you may include providing professional education. Your values may include financial security or this may take a very minor place in relation to a preferred value of living NOW with as much aliveness as you can create.

You must explore the things you want and had hoped for in this relationship. It is important to distinguish the valid needs from the "set-ups" which come from part of you that works against closeness. For example, when you are expecting your partner to provide experiences or emotions that another part of you is going to disclaim. This is also known as "drive your partner crazy" or "you can't win for losing."

There is currently a movement in the United States called *Marriage Encounter*. The central experience involves a weekend with other couples but most of the time is spent writing one's feelings on specific issues then sharing with one's partner and listening to him or her share. Bringing some of these feelings to awareness shatters marital boredom. It lifts the veil of familiarity and once more the mystery of the other is felt.

Most of us need quite a bit of practice in expressing our feelings. We don't do it easily and so we don't know ourselves too well.

The exercises suggested at the end of each chapter can help you start in your self-exploration. Some exercises are similar to those of marriage encounter, others were developed in my couple therapy groups with Dr. William M. Lamers and are designed to bring to the surface issues we find in many marriage crises.

I suggest you do these exercises alone. When you feel ready, share them with your partner. Don't defend what you have written. Share the feelings you have when you read what your partner has written. Ask him/her to tell you more. Respond, don't judge. Be as honest and real as possible, not what you wish you were. Share with your partner the times in your own experience when you felt as he/she feels. Describe back without evaluating what you hear your partner saying; bring out the depths. Real dialogue about feelings is an effort. You have to desire and want to understand, to get into the other's feeling consciousness. If you manage it you can bring a vital life and closeness into your relationship. We feel from the neck down. To reveal our inner feelings and reach out feels risky, but confidence comes partly when you make the decision to trust your partner and take this risk.

There are five stages to the process which can enable transformation of a crisis into rebirth of a relationship:

1. *awareness* that in certain situations and at certain times you feel quite uncomfortable in your marital interaction. The marriage is ineffective in meeting your own and your partner's needs.
2. *knowing what* feelings are actually there.
3. *redefining* your expectations and your sense of self-identity by integrating these feelings.
4. *rebuilding* your lifestyle with your partner.
5. *moving* toward more personal fulfillment within the possibilities and capacities that you sense between you.

Suggested Exercises

One place to begin is in finding the description below which makes you most uncomfortable in your marriage. Look over the following list. Perhaps there are several that seem familiar but pick the one which strikes your feeling response most strongly.

1. Not enough personal conversation. Our talk is surface, lifeless. It doesn't matter.

2. I feel moods of sadness and emptiness in our marriage.

3. We are indifferent to each other's problems and interests.

4. I feel disillusioned and bored with our relationship.

5. We don't fight. There is just no spark between us and there are occasions of coldness towards one another.

6. I (or my spouse) feel insecure and jealous. Another person interests me (or my partner) more.

7. There has been a lessening of courtesy, gentleness and signs of caring.

8. Other people understand me better than he/she does.

9. There is constant nagging or persistent bugging.

10. We don't plan things together.

11. Bad humor — something is always getting on his/her nerves.

12. I feel used.

13. I feel in a rut. We take each other for granted.

14. There are frequent quarrels or else insults, rudeness, teasing or sarcasm that passes for humor.

15. One or the other of us is continually escaping — TV, sports, compulsive socializing, liquor, hypochondria or else burying oneself in work or interest in the children.

16. There's no sense of mystery about one another and I feel little interest in wondering about him/her.

Now pick up a notebook and write everything you can think of in connection with this one area. Then go into your feelings and emotions, here and now, as you are recollecting instances. Check your body sensations, where you may feel constricted, held in, pressed down. Describe these awarenesses fully. Use adjectives and strong verbs to help define, describe, shape and color your feelings. Use analogies. "Having to keep this schedule, I feel gritty with anger." "When you come in the door, things begin to clear. It's like the sun on wet pavement."

Describe the attitude or state of mind that you associate with these feelings. Look at what you *think* causes it. Describe your behavior during these times. What position or point of view are you maintaining, e.g., are you identifying yourself as a helpless victim or as one who is running out on responsibilities? Do you know anyone from your past who took a similar stance? What feelings do you have in these times that you find most difficult to face in yourself?

Now go back to your complaint. Are you willing to give up your investment in keeping things the way they have been going? What state would you like to be in during those times? How can you bring this about? What would it cost?

For instance, in our example earlier Liz had to recognize that her present feelings of anger with Pete were really a cover for a less easily admitted wish for Pete's exclusive attention. In childhood she had a similar wish for her father's attention, but he was gone much of the time and never seemed to really notice her when he was there. So she had developed a sarcastic humor to hide her loneliness. Now she had to risk giving up the secondary rewards of a sharp tongue for the far more vulnerable position of admitting her wish to be loved — which wouldn't always be met.

The foregoing is a truth process and if you allow yourself to experience it fully, it will usually begin to erase your complaint as you recognize more aspects to the situation and your own involvement in it.

If it does not, then you must identify what it is that you want your partner to do. You must make an explicit demand of your partner. If you feel reluctant, what do you fear might happen? Does your fear justify your choice to hang onto the resentment? By this time though, you are probably more willing to talk to your partner because you sense your own strength in doing so. This exercise also will have helped you gain some awareness of an inner aspect of you that really doesn't want to get it together, a negative force in you that must be recognized and respected.

Chapter II

The Clash of Expectations —
The Crisis Exposed

Look back at some of your first meetings with people who have become important to you. Do you remember trying to impress her/him — showing the aspects of yourself that would probably please or charm? You may even have had some thoughts like "Can I be myself?" "I'm afraid I'll appear foolish." Excitement, anxiety, anticipation — do you remember how you saw the other person? As time went on, you probably became aware of more aspects in each other. Some of these you liked which made it easier to be together. Some, you possibly disliked which made for difficult times.

Many writers have suggested that within each of us there exists a multitude of personages, each one attempting to fulfill its own aims, sometimes cooperating but more often isolated or in a state of conflict. You might notice that you seem to be one person at work, another when vacationing with friends, another at home. Different aspects come to center stage and act as if that one aspect were "you" until the situation changes and another aspect is called forth.

Contemporary psychologists depict these subselves in various ways. Eric Berne's Transactional Analysis simplifies them to what he calls the five basic ego states—the nurturing parent, the critical parent, the adult, the adaptive child, and the natural child. How these subselves get along together and which state dominates within you has a lot to do with the conflicts and the pleasure that you experience with other people.

Carl Jung's Depth Psychology describes a number of entities. The personna is the official part that most people identify as you. The ego is the part of you that chooses and that *you* think of as you. Then there are a vast number of archetypal entities, including an aspect which is very like the opposite sex. This is called the anima (inner feminine) in a man and the animus (inner masculine) in a woman. According to Jungians, marriage always involves not only the relation between you and your partner but also the relation between these two inner aspects.

Fritz Perls, in Gestalt Psychology, confined himself to two major divisions of the personality usually found in conflict with one another. He called them top dog and underdog. The particular character and concerns of top dog and underdog vary from one person to another. But top dog always has very definite opinions about what underdog "should" be doing.

In literature, Stevenson's *Dr. Jekyll and Mr. Hyde* and Conrad's *Heart of Darkness* are among the many works that point to this same underlying reality. In each of us can be found all instincts, all vices and virtues and all tendencies of mankind. This is the basic empathy you feel for another person. You can directly understand another person through identifying with that part of yourself which is the same as he is. However, these common qualities are developed and active in you in various proportions which make you uniquely individual.

In practice there are some basic subpersonality constellations common to most people and it is on these facets that TA, Gestalt and Jungian psychology focus most effectively. Interventions based on them are quite often both effective and powerful in the hands of a skilled therapist. Nevertheless, it still is of major importance to consider your own unique personality without any expectation of finding the subpersonalities that fit any particular system. Look at your own unique formations, subsidiary responses and interactions.

You can find the subselves that belong to you alone. When you do gradually recognize them, you can begin to bring them to a closer order and harmony with a deeper sense of personal identity. Begin with your obvious roles to acquire this useful way of thinking.

Have you noticed that you behave differently in the office, in social situations, in church groups, when you are with your partner and when you are alone? Perhaps some people who know you only in one set of circumstances would be astonished if they could see you at home. But even with those persons closest to you—you act differently with your own mother than you do with your children and with your partner. Parts of you enter into each of these relationships that are not present in the others, perhaps a sternness with your children that you would not show to your partner or your parent, a sexuality with your partner that is not visible to your children, a filial quality with your parent that is not called for with your partner.

Each person has different "selves" according to the relationship he/she has with other people, surroundings, groups. It is important for you not to identify yourself with any *one* of these "selves" and to recognize that these are all roles that you play.

Your Cast of Characters

Think of yourself now in your various roles: as son or daughter, as husband or wife, as father or mother, as having a job of some kind, in the social and other roles you play or may want to play. In these roles, examine your

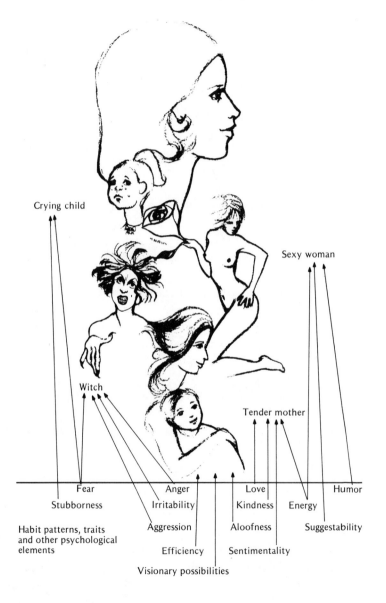

Crying child

Sexy woman

Witch

Tender mother

Fear   Anger   Love   Humor

Stubborness   Irritability   Kindness   Energy

Habit patterns, traits   Aggression   Aloofness   Suggestability
and other psychological
elements   Efficiency   Sentimentality

Visionary possibilities

from Elements Common to Every Person

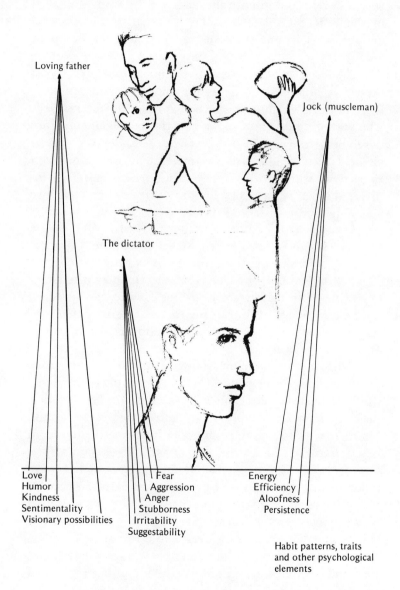

Loving father

Jock (muscleman)

The dictator

Love
Humor
Kindness
Sentimentality
Visionary possibilities

Fear
Aggression
Anger
Stubborness
Irritability
Suggestability

Energy
Efficiency
Aloofness
Persistence

Habit patterns, traits
and other psychological
elements

corresponding attitudes towards superiors, towards subordinates and towards your peers. You may discover you have very different and often quite antagonistic traits displayed in the different roles. It is not unusual to discover the defiant rebel in one situation can play top-dog tyrant in another.

A subself is a complex of habit patterns, traits and other psychological elements organized around an inner drive or urge which strives to be expressed, to be realized. The preceding diagram shows how the subpersonalities are developed from a pool of human traits and psychological elements that we all share. Certain traits cluster around an inner drive which then becomes a subpersonality. Your individual set of subselves, your inner cast of characters give you your unique style and flavor.

Once you turn your attention to them, you'll find a plethora of subselves—the Frightened Child, the Struggler, the Sexy Woman or Man, the Dummy, the Witch, the Controller-Grabber, the Crusader, the Doubter, the Great High One-Who-Knows, the Religious Fanatic, the Poisoner, the Tester, the Spiteful Brat, the Clown—many of them are in pairs of opposites and others relate in particular groupings to one another.

Julie, a young woman who grew up with a strong Rebellious Child, developed the Whore as an ally to the Rebel Child when she reached adolescence. Later in her twenties, she experienced a deeply meaningful religious conversion but there seemed now to be no room for her sexuality, so an inner character, Miss Priss, developed in the vacuum. The problem was Miss Priss picked aesthetically sensitive men to relate to who were not well grounded sexually, so none of the relations worked well. Julie's process of growing up had to harmonize and integrate the apparent opposites, the Whore and Miss Priss. Miss Priss had a fine sense of values except with sexuality. Whore had basically good sense about men and a wholesome sensuality which had been misallied with Rebel Child so her value was always discounted.

Julie had to first deal with the needs of Rebel Child for

attention and affirm her strong individuality then her need for affection before Miss Priss and Whore could merge and become sexual Woman. The subselves evolve and change as you relate to their needs more effectively.

There are in each of us a large number of these hidden personalities. Until you begin to identify them as such, parts — not the whole — distinct and separate from the essential "you," you are controlled by whatever subself you identify with in the moment (that which the situation has called forth in you). You have limited yourself to its particular good and bad qualities. As you identify the subpersonalities and relate to them as such, an integration becomes possible. You may have experienced an impasse or deadlock when two opposing drives or forces within you struggled for expression. You may have felt exhausted or empty without knowing that your energy was being drained by this head-on collision. Understanding this can lead to a means of expression where each of these personalities gets what it needs. As this process proceeds, gradually your deepest self, your true center becomes stronger.

Abe has a subself called the Rabbi made up of qualities of humanitarian concern and the visionary attributes of the mystic. He also has an efficient Businessman made up of aspects such as focus, willpower, drive and a shrewd sense of profit opportunities. Initially, the Rabbi and the Businessman, being so different from each other, were in constant conflict. They didn't understand and didn't like each other; each wanted to have its own way completely. They kept getting in each other's way, neither allowing the other to express itself freely and fully. Eventually Abe recognized them and organized a time-sharing so that he could have access to the qualities and strengths of both. This compromise was a major step toward his own integration. Initially he would only allow himself to be kind when he was identified with the Rabbi and efficient when he was into being the Businessman. Eventually a merger developed a more evolved subself — a kind, but efficient, humanitarian businessman.

What you want to do in recognizing the subselves is to

bring them into a state where they do not conflict but instead synthesize around a single personal *center* of identity. To best understand how opposite subselves can be reconciled, it is useful to understand how they arise. At one point in your development you may have strongly identified with one major subself and for all practical purposes believed yourself to be that part. Most of your energy flowed through the subpersonality. The other subselves developed more slowly without being recognized or accepted. You were therefore relatively free from conflict and felt o.k. *But* your aims were restricted to the particular aims of that subself and you were able to express only a small fraction of the qualities and gifts that are in you — those that the dominant subself accepts as its own.

Other traits the dominant subself simply filters out — *especially opposite qualities.* These qualities push for expression, however, and tend to seek, among other subselves, the one most akin. This is often found in a subself opposite to the dominant personality. It is as if the subselves were all within a single room which held only one outlet for expression. So long as the dominant subself does not want to give up its position of control, the way is blocked for the opposite subself to express itself directly. It may resort to manipulation or other devious maneuvers. In unusual circumstances, such as moments of stress, it can take over, take you by surprise and bring about a temporary shift in your identification.

Initially this may frighten you. You find yourself behaving in undesirable ways which you are unable to stop. In the earlier example of Julie, she identified herself as the Rebel child when she was only about 4 or 5 years old and she was seen by her family as that, a powerful reinforcement which blocked her other aspects from expression through most of her childhood. In adolescence, the Rebel subself accepted the Whore aspect as another expression of Rebel. What Rebel blocked from being seen was Julie's religious interests, sensitivity and truthful integrity. These initially took the form of subself, Miss Priss. When Julie was fully identifying herself as a Rebel and first became aware of Miss Priss's sensitivity and vision, she interpreted it as weakness and delusion to be ignored. But these tendencies became stronger and increasingly affected her behavior. The inner conflict between the two reached the conscious stage. For awhile she kept pushing away the new tendencies, postponing the issue which made it more difficult to deal with. She seemed unable to do anything, which is called the impasse phase in Gestalt therapy. Finally she experienced her religious conversion as an explosion. Miss Priss emerged into full consciousness with her many beautiful and valuable qualities which could now be expressed directly. This sudden release, and its corresponding flow of energy, she experienced as a peak of joy. It lasted until the stored energy was fully released.

But now Miss Priss wanted to stay in control and the Rebel was cut off. The energy flow through Rebel-Whore was now blocked in turn and pushed to be released. Soon these two began to fight each other for freedom of expression. This was apparent in the blocking of any effective relationship with the men in Julie's life. To Julie, now being identified with either subpersonality alone was unrewarding, inhibiting and a betrayal of a part of herself. She gradually became more identified with the conflict than with either subself.

This seemed to her to be a step back in her growth. She was unhappy and under stress. But her existence became increasingly uncomfortable and demanded the resolution of the conflict, the reconciliation of the two subpersonalities. So it was, in reality, a *transition* tward a higher level of integration, a definite step forward in her development.

Integration can be accomplished in different ways: *time-sharing* as in the example of Abe, in which each personality acts in the situations appropriate to it; *cooperation*—when the reasons for the conflict and the underlying needs are understood. The basic needs are often similar and the conflict is over the *means* to fulfill those aims. A close and fruitful cooperation is then possible.

Finally, as two or more subselves come closer together, eventually a merging occurs. There is a *fusion* resulting in a completely new subself. Julie's Rebel-Whore had a basic need for affection and her individuality to be affirmed. Miss Priss had a strong urge to express love in a religious response to her life and to other people. Understanding these basic needs allowed the fusion of the two subselves into a uniquely individual, compassionate, Sexual Woman.

As more and more subselves are harmonized and integrated, a deeper centered Self becomes apparent. Clearly individual, this Self behaves in ways characteristically responsible, caring and cooperative. An altruistic love becomes possible which goes beyond the aims of the individual and is more involved with all mankind.

Your Subselves in Interaction with Your Marriage Partner

Recognizing subselves can be very useful in your interactions with your marriage partner. For example, criticism is usually hard to accept because *we take it personally*. Once we speak and think in terms of subselves, the process is much easier. . . . "I think your Martyr is trying to make me feel guilty, do you agree?" Communicating in this way does not indicate "You're bad; you are at fault." It is a very straight message that one subpersonality may be out of control. We are responsible for our subpersonalities just as we are for our children. You do need to see that they don't cause trouble for yourself or to others. To the extent that you learn to work with this concept, it has the potential for doing away with a real stumbling block in couple communication — blame. It becomes you and I — and our subselves which we have to harmonize. We need to help each other in this because these characters inside give each other trouble when many of them could nurture and help each other.

For instance, I have a Frightened Child who was raised in the Great Depression of the thirties. When my husband seems concerned about his law practice or business matters, this part of me tends to go silent but runs with a "The sky is falling, Chicken-Little" message to my Super-Worker who then invades my professional life, overcommitting me to appointments, seminars and workshops. The Mystic and the Artist, with their tendencies to contemplate the universe, are banished. My husband encountering me, sees only the grim Worker. Another part of him hears the message that he is not taking care of me properly, and he should feel guilty. In addition, a part of him feels deprived and angry because he does not receive the comfort and understanding he has a right to expect.

When we recognized this set-up, a recurrent trouble area was detoxified in our relationship. I can catch myself when I start scheduling up time months in advance and go to him with "Hey, I need to talk to you. My Frightened Child has gotten into the works again. How are things with you?" I have learned that F.C. misreads a lot of signals. My husband has learned that I really trust him to care for me and I am around to care for him.

The early development of a subself and its initial struggle to express itself often occurs outside of your conscious awareness. You become aware of the situation only after a certain amount of development has taken place and, in some cases, only when you reach a crisis. If you can recognize newly emerging aspects sooner and understand their behavior and their needs, you can minimize conflict and foster your own growth and integration. It does not take much work to do this because it corresponds to your inner experience. What it takes is a quality of attention. The situation itself indicates which under-personalities need attention.

The acceptance of a subself and its coordination within your personality occur gradually. Positive aspects increasingly replace the negative but you must first accept the idea that the negative aspects are there before change can occur. Often you may reject a part of yourself that you dislike because you unconsciously believe that once you accept it, it will stay as it is forever. In reality, the opposite is true. When you reject that part of yourself, you create a block which increasingly distorts it and you are cut off from its useful qualities, skills and strengths. Once you accept it, you can discover the real needs of that personality. You can fulfill them in ways that are acceptable to you. It will release the positive qualities while transforming negative qualities into others more suitable. The appropriate filling of each subself's needs is a function of coordination. It is then possible for the subself to evolve and integrate harmoniously with the other aspects of your personality—and that of your partner.

When you first recognize aspects of yourself and of your partner, your attitude toward each of the aspects as towards people can vary, according to your values and your self-image. In general, people tend to accept a subself that is "good" according to their value system. One seen as "bad, harmful, or useless" is rejected. When you become aware of resisting a subself, it is sometimes useful to think of the Resister as another subself. Since you were identified with the resistance, you must step away from it. In not identifying with either, you can take the position of an unbiased objective observer.

The Gestalt technique differs in that it involves temporary identification with the subself which you reject. *Becoming* the subself brings an immediate experiential awareness of that subpersonality's existence. This, in turn, can lead to a compassionate understanding of its needs, the reasons for its attitudes, and then to its acceptance. In the top dog/underdog dialogue, for instance, you alternatively identify first with one and then with the other, stating the position and needs of each and creating a dialogue between the two. If this does not lead the conflicting parts to a cooperative understanding, you as the objective observer, enter the discussion to bring about a resolution.

Whenever you go deep enough into the core of a subself you will find that there is some basic need or urge that is good. If it became twisted it was because it was not able to express itself directly. The basic purpose of the objective observer is to discover this central urge or need, to make it conscious and to find acceptable ways in which it can be fulfilled, satisfied and grow. If it cannot really be satisfied, then you must find an agreeable compromise. But a little bit of satisfaction goes a long way. When subselves are repressed, they get nothing, and when they get nothing, they want everything. For instance, if you discover a subself in you that behaves like a 4 year old, it is probably in you because it has not really been "fed" since *you* were 4 years old. When you take care of it, it will grow up, then gradually it will begin to work with you.

Your partner or you may have a "dictator" subself. The dictator wants power and may want to rule everyone in sight . . . beginning with you. In trying to understand the reason behind this you must go toward more and more basic needs. Like some people, a subself of this kind wants power because at some time it was not able to have love, needed it and did not know how to ask for it directly. But he/she knew how to get power and with power tries to force substitutes for love. If you recognize that under the need for power there is often the need for love, you can straighten things out. You can say, essentially, "I can't let you run or manipulate me but I can love as you stop misusing power. I can see you're starved for love and don't know how else to go about getting it. I can see you do know a lot about power but there are other ways I would like to have you use it."

Developing and relating to the subselves is part of a deeper process in which these aspects are transformed. From a general state of isolation, conflict, competition and repression of the weaker elements by the stronger ones they can move to a state of cooperation. In *this new state* each aspect finds the space and nourishment it needs to develop fully. Once you are capable of not identifying yourself with any or all of them at will, these inner aspects of yourself will blend their useful and valuable qualities with each other. Gradually you form an integrated, individual personality. You no longer will have to deal with rigid formations. The qualities and energies will become freely available to you to fit each new situation.

The following illustration indicates that there are times

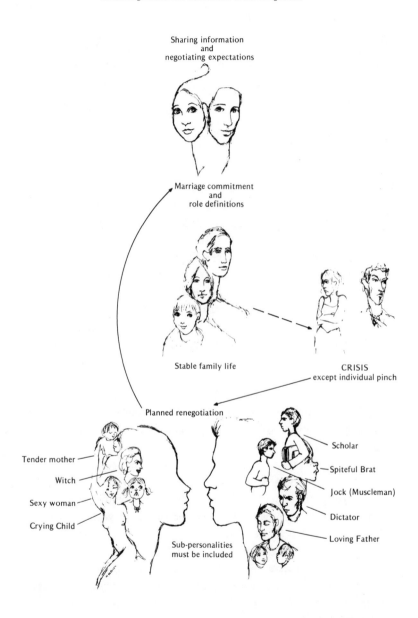

Sharing information
and
negotiating expectations

Marriage commitment
and
role definitions

Stable family life

CRISIS
except individual pinch

Planned renegotiation

Tender mother

Witch

Sexy woman

Crying Child

Scholar

Spiteful Brat

Jock (Muscleman)

Dictator

Loving Father

Sub-personalities
must be included

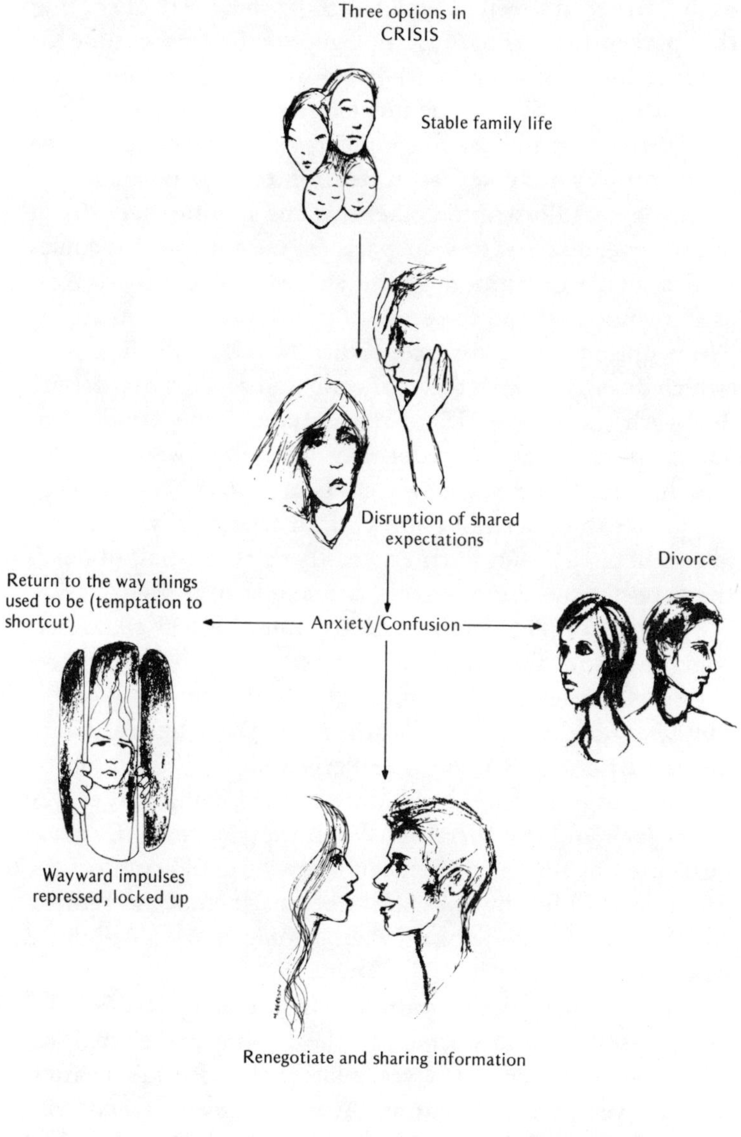

Three options in
CRISIS

Stable family life

Disruption of shared
expectations

Return to the way things
used to be (temptation to
shortcut)

Divorce

Anxiety/Confusion

Wayward impulses
repressed, locked up

Renegotiate and sharing information

when you or your partner feel your needs are not being cared for in the marriage as it is. The different subselves in each partner are seen. There has to be some way of sharing this perception. You must renegotiate for more time or space or for satisfaction of whatever need you become aware. Since these needs may be the expression of inner subself voices, the first illustration indicates some work has to be done within you as well as in relation to your partner.

The next illustration takes this one step further. If you fail to renegotiate with your partner, inevitably crisis comes with a sharp disruption of the shared expectations. Now anxiety increases and the sense of personal confusion grows. Three options open: divorce, return to the way things were (which does away with the confusion and anxiety but doesn't deal with the issues) *OR* to renegotiate. Renegotiation involves going back to redefining why you want to live together and what you now understand your needs to be.

You can understand how certain aspects of you emerge in conflicts with your partner. Mostly this is a result of needs that are not met because they are not seen as such.

For example, Paula has an inner set of characters which include: the Engineer, the Sexy Woman, the Prosecuting Attorney, the Frightened Child, the Responsible Mother and the Fearless Truth-sayer. Dan, her husband, has the Brightest Scholar, the Perfect Child ("I can do no wrong"), the Unappreciated Martyr, the Loving Father, the Super Jock and the Dictator. When they married, Dan was fascinated by the Sexy Engineer, knew he could comfort the Frightened Child, but was a bit nervous around the Fearless Truth-sayer. He anticipated Paula would make a delightful wife and mother.

Paula enjoyed the company of the Brightest Scholar and Super Jock and warmed to the Loving Father in Dan. How does it happen, ten years later, that Paula's Fearless Truth-sayer and Prosecuting Attorney have clashed with Dan's Unappreciated Martyr and Dictator? One principal reason is Paula's unrecognized need for certainty. The other is Dan's lack of recognition of his shadow side and power drive.

The roots lie in the past. Paula survived a childhood with many difficulties, primarily because she could trust her mind to figure things out. She did not have to be frightened by her mother's fears but could determine what the facts were. She learned to analyze carefully. She couldn't let herself be swayed by emotional people because they would confuse the picture with frightening possibilities.

Dan, on the other hand, grew up in a family system which contained no fearsome surprises. Everything was smoothly under control. Feelings were well-regulated and low key without conflict. No one would dream of making anyone else uncomfortable by asking him to do something he did not wish to do. Dan, himself, was viewed as the perfect son.

In their relationship, trouble developed when Paula's need for certainty led her to complex analyses of many situations. Dan began to feel totally hemmed in, without the freedom for any spontaneous, much less risky choices. He was used to managing relationships in such a way that no overt conflict would develop. He sacrificed many of his own wishes without drawing Paula's attention to this. She did not realize that he was, in fact, giving up his own preferences and inwardly growing more resentful. Eventually, in self-defense, he simply did not give overt recognition that he was hearing what she had to say. She in turn, feeling unheard, escalated her messages. She sent them over and over, feeling increasingly frantic that she was not being heard.

The relationship progressed from one with a rich mixture of possibilities to one in which Paula's Prosecuting Attorney and her Fearless Truth-sayer assumed control. Dan, having tried and failed with his self-sacrificing Loving Father, then retreated into being the Unappreciated Martyr. He finally became solely the Dictator who refused to give Paula's messages any recognition. He did not admit that he was now, in fact, running the show his way.

In the renegotiation phase, both Paula and Dan had to dis-identify with these inner characters and get back to what needs they actually represented. How they did this is described in Chapter V.

You could not share all the information you would need for your life together with your partner when your relationship first began. For one thing, certain aspects of you come into being only as the relationship unfolds. The other aspects not shared are unvoiced expectations, hopes, assumptions, your fantasies of the ideal mate, and projections of some of your own qualities onto one another. Later as you fill the role of husband, the role of wife, the role of parent, new aspects of you develop. Society's pressures, economic realities and the tasks of each phase of life further define your experience of yourself. Men in their work generally expand their knowledge, exercise their talents and have an increased number of social contacts. These are sources of self-esteem as the years go by in their work roles. Women's roles have often involved shrinking their interests to home and children and leaving their nonfamily skills unused and undeveloped. Our society has not placed high value on the complex tasks of raising children, running a household, acquiring and using possessions well. Today a woman is usually the first to feel and express the individual pinch. Becoming aware of this pain and valuing it as a signal for needed attention is the essential first step in the evolution and maturation of your marriage.

Suggested Exercises

Your work with exercises in the previous chapter has probably given you a feeling for some of your subselves. Now you may feel ready to identify them explicitly and increase your awareness of how they operate within you.

The following method is one I used 12 years ago when I first started to explore the notion of myself as an inner group:

If you type, sit at a typewriter and address a question that concerns you to yourself. Listen, type the answer which occurs to you, then type your response. If you don't type, write it out. Listen again and add any afterthoughts that occur to you. Continue in this fashion, stopping each time so that no one "voice" monopolizes the conversation. When you have reached a stopping place, ask "Is there anyone else who would like to be heard?" Listen, type and continue the conversation until it feels concluded.

When you have finished, read over what you have written. How many voices do you discern? Name them. Is there one which interests you more than the others, perhaps an unexpected voice? Ask it what it *wants,* and why. Ask it what it *needs,* and why. Now let yourself become this subself. What is the world like to you now? Ask yourself what you would like to do. What would my life be like if I were to embody this aspect of me all the time? How do I feel about my marriage partner? What do I want from him/her? What do I need from him/her?

Now take another look at the subself and examine carefully what you like and what you dislike about what you see. Try to reach an understanding with it.

Repeat the exercise on another occasion with the same character or different ones. Examine any recurrent marriage relationship problems from the point of view of these inner subselves. Consult your partner about how he/she sees these different aspects of you. Invite him/her to discover his/her characters and the interplay between his/her characters and your own.

Chapter III

How Did We Get to This Point?

Of the many factors which influenced you in choosing your mate, probably the most obvious is the fact that you were around one another for a sufficient length of time to make some assessments. Continuing with the idea of subselves, developed in the last chapter, it is as if each aspect of your inner group had been scanning your "dates" as potential candidates for some time to see if you would "fit" together. One way to think of relationships is by creating a sculpture. A sculpture must have an overall shape but the individual parts relate to one another to bring out this design. You will see this in the examples which follow and you will also begin to glimpse your own family sculpture.

Different members of your inner group had varying degrees of enthusiasm for possible partners. The one you chose probably had the backing of a coalition of subselves in you although there may have been one or two dissenting voices. For instance, Liz met Pete in college. Liz was an only child. Her mother was a member of the D.A.R., her father a wealthy businessman who had gone broke twice. He still "made it" sufficiently to give his daughter a good education. Family values were pure WASP (white, Anglo-Saxon, Protestant American). Liz had an inner group of subpersonalities: Proper Daughter, Perverse Child, The Entertainer, The Reader, The Mother and The Sexpot. Pete was Irish-Catholic, the ambitious only son from a large family. He was intelligent, popular, a "big-man-on-campus." Liz's Proper Daughter self could clearly see that Pete was going to be financially successful and provide her with the life-style and setting she and Entertainer wanted. The Perverse Child and The Mother in her for the first time in her life were gleefully in accord—Perverse Child thought she could finally get back at her parents whose values were anti-Catholic and anti-large family. The Mother in her was delighted at the prospect of never being lonely again because she could have a huge family. Only Sexpot was a bit skeptical. Pete looked fairly stodgy to her. How about having some fun? She had another candidate in mind but Proper Daughter vetoed that and the choice was Pete.

Pete, on the other hand, had an inner cast of characters also—Horatio Alger was dominant, the Renaissance Man with a tremendous range of interests came second, then followed the Charmer-Politician, the Pirate and the Responsible Accountant (viewed sometimes by his younger sisters as Tight-fisted Scrooge). Horatio subself thought Liz "the right girl from the right family" and a proper mother for his children. Renaissance Man recognized her Intelligent Reader would appreciate him. Charmer-Politician and Pirate were male chauvinists but intrigued by Sexpot and Perverse Child. Only Responsible Accountant had reservations about "that girls's expensive tastes" so Pete's choice was Liz.

So what happened? Having "fallen in love," they married and embarked on raising the large family they both wanted. Pete was very successful indeed. He rose to the top of his company; he charmed away the prejudices of Liz's family. In fact, Perverse Child began to notice that Pete and her parents had an awful lot in common, notably they wanted their own way about everything—so she began to think in perverse ways to get back at *him*. Proper Daughter and the Entertainer merged to become Social Hostess. She still was hugely pleased with Pete so long as they were in public. In private she was banished by the Mother who regarded Pete as a nuisance to be endured for the sake of the children. Sexpot still didn't have any place of her own, as everyone ignored her, including Pete. His Horatio Alger and Renaissance Man subselves were busy sulking at being unappreciated. The Charmer-Politician who could see that Liz enjoyed him in public was baffled by her unresponsiveness in private. He felt displaced by his children and retired with three quick martinis when he entered the house, leaving his shoes to be filled by Accountant-Scrooge who threatened, hollered and carried on in high style, but felt very, very empty inside.

The crisis came with the school truancy of their oldest son. As so often is the case, the child's behavior was the signal of family distress. When the family came into treatment, the opportunity was created for Pete and Liz to look at the position they were in and how unsatisfying to each of them it was.

Some inner and outer shifting of power takes place. Liz's Perverse Child has independent spunky strength. This gradually links up to the wide ranging interests of Reader who has tended to be a passive spectator, but now may be evolving into a highly individual woman, fully equal to Renaissance Man. Sexpot, so long suppressed, is making a few tentative moves as Charmer and Renaissance Man displace the Accountant in the bedroom. The children understand much about these matters without it ever having to be worded and are now free to go about their own affairs and get on with creating their own lives.

Many years of gradual drifting structured the marriage relationship you have, even as it did with Pete and Liz. We have used a simple technique which can increase your understanding of your own patterns of behavior. Perhaps you can see how they were originally structured and the ways in which they are taking you, unless you redesign them with your choices based on satisfying your present needs.

When you were a child you got a lot of messages and instructions about the kind of person you were to become from your family. You learned how to dress, what friends to choose and your parents' attitudes toward life, particularly their view of your worth, your importance or lack of it. These instructions had a lot to do with creating the various aspects of you inside that we have been calling the subselves. You are now going to investigate how you came to think about yourself in the ways you do, perhaps how you limit yourself in the ways you do. You want to clear away distortions picked up from how other people have viewed you and how you have responded. You now want to reach a sense of deciding your own place in your marriage, setting your own goals with all the facets of you and of your partner to be included and cared for.

Using an art process can help loosen your ordinary ways of thinking and allow different aspects of you to be expressed. The following process involves the use of clay or play-doh. It is best if both you and your partner each work on your family sculpts during the same period because the implications for your marriage become clear in the process of analysis.

*The Family Sculpture**

Materials you will need: a good double handful of clay, paper and pencil.

First, close your eyes and go back to a time in your childhood, somewhere between two and eight years old. Think about the members in your

* From *The Inward Journey: Art as Therapy for You,* Margaret Keyes.

family. Who was around? How old were they? How did you feel about them?

Note on the paper two or three adjectives describing each person. Take the clay and make a sculpture of the adjectives describing one particular person, e.g., if you described Dad as warm but critical, you might make just an arm reaching out from a ball with a lot of sharp points. The idea is not to make a figure of a person, but something that gives a feeling of how that person felt to you when you were younger.

When you have sculpted each family member in turn, put them in relation to each other to show who felt close and who was far away from you emotionally. You might show who was on top and who was under someone else in the family.

You now have a sculpture that shows what it felt like to be growing up in the family into which you were born. Look at it carefully and sense what your sculpture might indicate that you had not thought of before. Write one question or comment from each family member in the sculpture to you, and then your comment or question to each family member.

You can discover how your inner aspects developed in looking at the messages from family members and the decisions you made about them. The messages you wrote from the sculpture are some of the instructions you received about what you should do to gain approval and what you should avoid. Some of the problematic messages had to do with *not* being you: "Be perfect." "Don't be silly." "Don't be a child." To whatever degree your own parents were hurt, confused, felt inadequate or frightened, they may have sent you limiting messages along with their good advice.

As a child you learned to behave in ways that got you

some attention. Even if it was not the kind you wanted most, some was better than none, so your family directives on how to get it mattered to you. Certain feelings or actions were associated with that attention, getting on the honor roll or playing dumb, throwing a tantrum, becoming a rebel or playing a victim to feel justified. Any one of these could have become a favorite role for manipulating the attention you needed. As such, that role represents the child form of a subself you now know, e.g., the Achiever, the Dummy, the Rebel.

A good clue in understanding your own functioning is to think about the problematic feeling with which you are most familiar — competition, jealousy, anger, depression or grim determination. It might be a feeling that you used to associate with some kind of attention in your family. If showing angry feelings in your family didn't work because they were coldly ignored, you may have learned to play Helpless Victim which at least made someone feel guilty enough to respond to you. Today you might find that when you are tempted to tears of helplessness, you are hiding a fury of anger inside. Why hiding? Largely because the feeling of anger is still unacceptable to another part of you, much like that family member who wouldn't accept your anger originally.

You have just looked at the clay sculpture as it depicts the emotional climate of the actual family in which you grew up and the directions you received from the family on how to be you. Now, assuming these instructions provided you with a program on how to live your life, you can look at the circumstances and the people in your present life to check out whether this is so.

Look at the family sculpture for the feelings it sets up in you; then go over the list of instructions from family members on how to be, how to act in getting attention and managing your life. Who is sending these messages to you now? How many do you experience as coming from your partner? Can you identify the times and ways in which you send these messages to yourself? It is almost incredible how many people find all, or nearly all of the early messages now sensed as coming from their spouse and from their work. They appear either in the form of professional standards or from the actual person who is "boss." If you discover there is a strong carry-over, you are in a position to clear away some of the major distortions in your relationships.

Family Sculpts of Liz and Pete

Liz's Family

MOTHER—"has all the answers" "busy" "social"

FATHER—"charming, but absent" "sportsman"

LIZ—"interested" "squashed down" "bookish"

Messages:

Mother to Liz: "Work hard, but no matter how hard you
  work you won't please me." "Mother knows best."
  "You'll always be a little inadequate in my eyes."
Father to Liz: "You're O.K. but don't count on me."
Liz to Mother: "I'll conform on the outside but inside you
  can't make me and I'll sabotage you."
Liz to Father: "I won't let myself know I need you."

Pete's Family

FATHER—"strong
opinions, competent
and hardworking"

MOTHER—"self-
sacrificing, religious,
a good woman"

GRANDPARENTS AND AUNTS—
        "good, upright, honest
        and hardworking"

YOUNGER SISTERS—
"mischief makers, annoying"

PETE—"bright, top of
class, many interests"

Messages:

Father and Mother to Pete: "You're a winner." "Work hard
    and we'll be proud of you."
Grandparents and Aunt: "You have what it takes."
Sisters to Pete: "Give me!"
Pete to parents: "I'll go to the top."
Pete to relatives: "I agree."
Pete to sisters: "O.K., but get off my back."

> In looking at the family sculpts, it is clear where
> some of the problem areas would tend to be be-
> tween Pete and Liz. Liz's family allows for more
> individuality in contrast to Pete's rather mono-
> lithic conformity. Liz's program calls for secret
> rebellion against an oppressor who has "all the
> answers" and Pete's center-stage self clearly holds
> that possibility. His feminine personages, on the
> other hand are seen as either self-sacrificing or
> annoying! A further difficulty can be seen in that
> Liz early learned she couldn't depend on mascu-
> line support to help her with self-assertion.

Liz was dismayed to realize that she was sending the same
messages she had received as a child now to her husband:
"Work hard but no matter how hard you work you won't be
able to please me." "Mother knows best." "You'll always be
a little inadequate in my eyes." Her other family messages
had stressed proper behavior, keeping up appearances, a
duty to be sociable so that time to one's self was frowned on.
Overt anger, of course, was inconceivable in such an atmosphere. She had, in other words, an inner character very
much like her own mother who sometimes spoke with Liz's
voice to Pete and sometimes to Liz herself, not letting her
have "idle" time.
    Pete's family messages structured his life in terms of

success and winning at work, but no particular attention was given to sex and implicitly it was understood that "women don't count for much except in raising children and running the home."

Pete and Liz each had life programs which meshed well insofar as living a socially oriented and financially successful life. They also managed fairly well as parents. Where the pinch was felt was in their personal relationship. Neither had received either approval of their sexuality or family role models of healthy affection and well-grounded sensuality. Their sexual life lacked a natural zest. In addition, Liz had a program which called for hidden anger so issues between them were never really resolved. She also failed to give herself the time that she needed to develop her separate non-social interests which would have allowed other forms of delight in her life. Pete's male chauvinism went unchallenged as it provided a handy excuse for her hidden anger and a version of the "If It Weren't For You" game. When she recognized this, she could begin to take responsibility for her own life again, deciding what she wanted to put her time into and how to allow various inner aspects to develop. Pete too, had to decide to use his resources differently and how to enable underdeveloped aspects within him to emerge. For example, in discounting women, he had also discounted aspects of himself which had a perspective he needed in order to become less driven.

Marriage partners use a variety of ways to relate to one another. For some couples, it is basically satisfying for one or the other to play Wise Parent to the other person's inner Child. Some marriages are structured in terms of common values and agreement on the shoulds and oughts of life. "We are here to serve the Lord's Will." Others depend on the collusion of two lonely children, "the world's a frightening place and all we have in life is each other" or two fighters, "the world is a place to be conquered and overcome."

The current lack of certainty in role definitions contributes to the unease in some of today's marriages. To the extent the couple involved are personally clear about their interaction and the way they define the fit of their roles together, personal security and marital development can result. By using the notion of subpersonalities, you can pinpoint where some of the difficulties may lie in your marital relationship and you can identify what needs to happen.

Clearly a relationship which satisfies only one or two aspects in each partner can survive if these aspects are strong and central. It is more likely to be productive and satisfying to the degree that more of your subpersonalities are well related and involved with one another and with your partner. Even in a marriage which has a good solid core of agreement, however, difficulty comes when one or more unsatisfied aspects come to dominate the interaction.

For an example, Roxanne was the oldest child of an achievement oriented Russian Jewish immigrant father. He delighted in her quick intellect even as he disparaged his son's slowness. Rather than showing this directly, however, he pushed her to become the great concert pianist he had longed to be but had sacrificed for business success. Roxanne was extremely responsive to beauty in any dimension—not only music, but colors, textures, the complexity of the design of plants, the excitement of patterns in mathematics.

The problem was that all of this, including her rich, sensual fantasy life had gone underground as the pressure mounted for her to perform in the ways that her father valued. She pushed herself to overcome her terror in recitals by going into a state of numbness in which she played automatically. Any anger or resentment she might have felt was thoroughly repressed in fear of her father's anger. She did not feel seen or valued except in this automaton role. Her mother had given her the strong message that she was no beauty and had better make it with as little rocking the boat as possible.

Growing up, she gradually unfolded some of her inner interests and, in fact, was seen by many who worked with her as remarkably interesting. Howard, a young physics teacher from an austerely Puritan background, had a buried poet within him. He was strongly drawn to her, sensing in her a capacity for sensuality and joy that he lacked and for which he hungered. They were married and the marriage had moments of great richness. Gradually as the young man advanced in his career, his energies more and more were diverted into his intellectual interests. Roxanne had given up her separate career and took pleasure in her children. But she increasingly felt a sense of being invisible, such as she had as a child — and valued only for her performance — the good cook and hostess, household manager and mother. The artist and the musician were no longer seen. She became aware of her anger, but as in childhood it was linked with powerlessness. She felt bound to perform. She hungered to be touched, seen and delighted in, and she knew she had all these inner riches. With her husband's apparent blindness, she felt discounted. Her hunger expressed itself in oversmoking, overeating and she grew to reject her own body, reinforcing her mother's assessment that she was no beauty. Soon it seemed that the only part of her that her husband could see was a silent reproachful bristly woman whose signals for love he could not read. He in turn felt vaguely guilty as he had with his cold mother and this called out in him the escapist response it had as a child. He buried himself further in his books. The poet again was lifeless.

Breaking this kind of pattern, where two opposing subselves unable to relate to one another have been set up in the partners, requires individual work. Each person has to recognize that he/she is principally relating to the partner from one problematic aspect. This in turn he/she has to identify and relate to in him/herself. Roxanne had to recognize her silent, conforming but angry child and ask it what it wanted. Then she had to clarify what it needed. She had to think also of ways in which she could help these needs to be met rather than continuing her own repression of her inner child's sensitive responses on the grounds that she could only come out if her husband valued her.

Transactional Analysis condenses the many subselves into the three ego-states of Parent, Adult and Child. Parent is when you find yourself reacting to a person or a situation as you once experienced your own parents acting, either in a critical or nurturing way. Adult is when you are objectively computing or responding. Child is when you are reacting with the strong surviving natural feelings and responses you had as a child, or in the adaptive way you learned as a child to hide your feelings. In these terms the situations of Pete and Liz could be diagramed in this way:

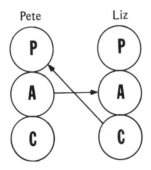

When Pete would think he was being objective and reasonable and Liz would react to his messages as if they were coming from a critical parental "I know what's best" ego state. The transaction would cross and communication was cut off. Pete was left with a feeling "No matter what I do I'm not appreciated," a dejected parental state. Liz experienced a triumphant, defiant "You think you're so powerful but you can't make me" adaptive perverse child state.

Roxanne and her husband Howard's situation could be diagramed in the same way. The difference was that Roxanne's silent withdrawal activated Howard's confused, inadequate child feelings so they both were left with the familiar problematic feelings they each had felt as children. Until the real needs of each person under these feelings can be identified and met, the situation tends to repeat and repeat itself. Pete yearns to be stroked and appreciated. Liz needs to acknowledge her own autonomy. Roxanne longs to be accepted unconditionally for what she is rather than for what she does, and Howard needs to experience and value his own adequacy which can only come when he allows himself to be responsive.

Internally what each needs to do is to connect the more nurturing aspects of his/her own Parent ego state with the deprived child within:

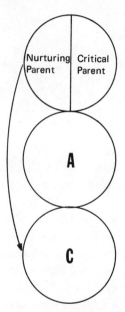

The potential we each have for nurturing is most often used in relation to others rather than ourselves. Self-rejection of some aspect of one's personality is the root of all neurosis. Of course, there is a little secret "if only" hope connected to this. If only *someone else* would see and value this aspect of me, I would be transformed. Beauty kisses Beast and the handsome young man is released from his spell. The princess kisses the frog and he changes into a Prince. The ugly duckling grows up and someone else recognizes he is a swan.

People enter marriage and therapy with some of these same unacknowledged hopes—that "someone else will do it for me, will see and love me for what I am."

A marriage can be satisfying when one person plays nurturing parent to the other's needy child. If this is the dominant role, however, it is highly constricting, and usually means that something is stuck in the relationship.

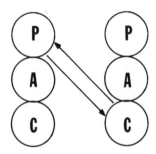

For instance, Frank and Sally had a relationship in which she literally felt smothered by his kindness, and he felt depressed by her ingratitude. She remembered that she had always been able to "manage" her difficult father, but the cost was to always appear pretty and cheerful and never let any other feelings show. Now, it seemed to her that when her husband was kind to her, he also was demanding. She never showed any negative feelings. If she did, he would get depressed. Thus, she felt only the choice to do this, or to smother her feelings as she had with her father. He in turn, but unknown to her, was struggling with parental messages from his own parents that no matter how hard he tried, it would never be enough.

Although he did not intend to cut his wife off from expression of negative feelings, this was the effect because he would try to please her as he had tried to please his parents. When she protested that it was too much, he was overprotective, overly generous, he would once more feel the depression that he had felt as a child. "Nothing he could do would ever be enough"—an apparently hopeless situation until they could get an adult-to-adult clarity. What Frank wanted from Sally was not a "pretty doll" wife, but a woman who would freely love him *and* also could disagree with him and have her own interests and points of view. What Sally felt toward Frank was not that he was inadequate and not capable of pleasing her—far from it. She valued all his signs of care so long as they did not mean she couldn't have her negative feelings.

The more aspects of each partner that can successfully relate to aspects in the other partner, the richer the marriage, so that when indicated, each is comfortable in parenting the other:

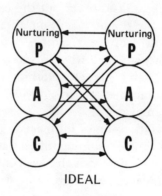

IDEAL

The two can compute and plan and share interests in an adult state and each is free to bring his/her playful child and know the other will be fun to do things with. The importance of a playful child relationship can't be overstated as a sign of a healthy creative marriage.

One sure sign of a marriage in trouble is the WALL OF TRIVIA* which is built up bit by bit. It surely and inevitably cuts off first the child ego state of each partner from the other and finally the two adult ego states so only the two critical parents can look over the wall:

*The WALL OF TRIVIA is a concept developed by Transactional Analyst Mary Goulding.

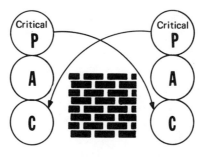

WALL OF TRIVIA

Each brick in the wall is an accusation usually phrased as a generalization, e.g., "You never put the cap on the toothpaste," to which the response is "You always expect me to pick up after you drop your clothes around everywhere after work." "Oh yeah, well who do you think does all the shopping around here?" etc. etc. Nothing is ever answered. No one point has merit except as a device in the "I'm right; you're wrong" game.

The deep relationship of intimacy is tremendously rewarding but it is time consuming, often uncomfortable and difficult to sustain. It demands that we continually work toward our own wholeness. So many of us avoid intimacy and play the games of our partial selves instead. TA has identified many of these games. I'll only describe one which I've found to be the most prevalent—"IF IT WEREN'T FOR YOU. . . ." "If it weren't for you insisting on having a baby, I could have completed law school." "If it weren't for you rushing me to get married, I could have played around more and really experienced what other men/women were like." "If it weren't for you, I could have gone on with my career and become a great ballet star." The point to note is that almost always the complainer has some secret doubts about whether in fact he had the stamina to make it through law school, whether in fact he/she could attract other men/women or whether she had the talent and dedication to put up with the long hours of practice necessary in ballet.

This game makes it possible to hold the fantasy "I could have been great" without testing it and to blame the other thereby, "being right." It successfully avoids confronting the secret self-doubts and the whole issue of the cost that would have been involved in a genuine choice.

Suggested Exercises

Because you bring to your present experience with your partner feelings and attitudes shaped by your past, you may now want to explore together some of the facts of your past life to find how these influence your relationship.

Complete for each other the following sentences with the first thing that comes to mind:

> My childhood . . .
> Father was the kind of man who . . .
> He usually . . .
> He and I . . .
> Mother can best be described as . . .
> She usually . . .
> Mother and I . . .
> I was happiest when . . .
> I got angry when . . .
> I felt blue when . . .
> Family meals were times when . . .
> On my birthday . . .
> On Sundays . . .
> When I was ill . . .
> I used to look . . .
> In school . . .
> With other children my own age . . .
> When I had my first wet dream . . .
> When I first menstruated . . .
> When I first heard how babies were made . . .
> I was told that playing with myself would . . .

I used to daydream that . . .
I never realized that . . .
At night I . . .
When I did something wrong . . .
I had a friend who . . .
When I was between 3 and 6 years old . . .
Between 6 and 10, I . . .
When I was between 10 and 15 . . .
In my spare time I liked best to . . .

As you look over these feeling facts now, does anything surprise you? Do any connections occur to you with your current life and that of your partner? Now, describe yourself in the present. What are your good points, your bad points? What do you find most attractive about your partner, what you like best about yourself? What feeling do you find most difficult to share with your partner, what feeling is most difficult to face in yourself?

There are some useful rules to observe when you share with one another. Don't explain, just describe. Be as open, honest and trusting as you can, and accept the other's effort in the same spirit.

The next exercise is difficult and it is best done in a context that allows you to be both giving and confronting. For instance, if you enjoy a foot massage, you might take turns giving a massage while asking the following questions. When you have finished, your partner does the same for you.

How do you avoid me?
What do you fear in me?
What do you resent in me?
What are you not telling me?
How do you control me?
What would you like from me?
How do you block us off from one another?
As you look at me now, what do you see?

It is important that you ask the questions in an open, receptive way and listen without attempting to deny, defend or explain. When you both have finished you can share with one another what the experience has meant to you.

Chapter IV

Marital Problem Analysis

The most popular methods of marriage therapy stress the importance of proper technique in communication. However, I find that some people can communicate clearly with one another, know their own feelings and acknowledge the other's, and still have problems in their relationship. These problems are often rooted in different values, different ways of experiencing, perceiving and assessing issues. This chapter briefly explores the five problem areas most frequently discussed in couple therapy — money, power-control, sex and affection, children, and alcohol.

Money

Money provides an amazing symbolic system to express the problems of value, of being valued and of valuing. It is measurable and easier to talk about than the feelings that surround its use. Sometimes with a couple therapy group or a class of students, I suggest an experiment: Everyone is to take out the small change they carry and count it, then without words to distribute as much or as little as they choose to everyone else in the group. That done, I now suggest they put their collection in front of them and again go round, this time taking as much as they choose from each person's collection. Some distribute equally to everyone, others give varying amounts to indicate their esteem and then watch very closely to see who gives to them. Very few realize that they do not have to give and even when they do, they feel group pressure to at least minimally participate. When it comes to taking, feelings are even more varied. One plays Robin Hood, taking only from the "rich," another takes nothing, a third carefully takes only what he put out, another gleefully pirates as much as he can hold. It is a game, but in the discussion afterwards, the underlying values usually reflect the attitudes each person holds concerning money.

Money is linked with power and, therefore, control. Money often substitutes for love or acceptance. Many people assess their own self worth in terms of how much they make in comparison to others. This conditions an attitude for women who give lesser value to mothering and household work and to volunteer rather than paid work. A student in her late thirties describes her situation: "As a non-wage earning housewife, I feel my contribution in mothering, caring for the home and accompanying responsibilities is not equally valued even though it would cost to hire someone to do it. I fight this attitude like Hell and keep looking for articles listing the monetary values of household services but there still exists in me a feeling that I have not made it in the real world."

Marriage has a fundamental economic base. Much household time is taken up with practicalities that involve money, shopping, paying bills, preparing meals, tasks that keep the household running. Today, households are not being run well for many reasons. Runaway inflation means that there is less to manage on. More women are working and this means they have less time to manage their money and the household tasks. With the present state of the economy, most people are aware that these problems have social rather than personal causes. But personal feelings get attached, for example, self-pride in being a good provider, in knowing how to manage.

Inflation and income loss are serious threats to household and personal security for millions today.

Even the wealthiest households are into money issues when investments "go sour" and there is a lack of certainty in planning for the future. Many of us with personal histories of family losses during the Great Depression of the thirties have conflicting and contradictory feelings about money. We feel a need to scrimp and save and get the most for our money. At the same time, throughout most of our adult years we have accepted our cultural role as consumers. Our economy pushes people to buy more than they actually need. Few of us wait until we can pay cash. What is important is a regular monthly payment setup with no real question about total cost, comparative interest rates or real need. We have become a society of people constantly in debt and always wanting more.

Blaming the partner for not providing enough, or for not managing well what is provided, obscures some of these basic issues. The current moves toward consumer boycotts, "consumer conspiracy" buying co-ops and legislative advocates gives some social recognition to the problems a family is facing financially. On the individual level, partners need to acknowledge, in fact, that money is in short supply and family priorities have to be thought about. Buying a home and making payments may now be out of reach for many middle income families, not only the poor. The use of energy, of gasoline, of "convenience" foods and supplies formerly taken for granted have to be looked at in terms of their relative costs and necessity. The meaning of money to each partner and its use has to be rethought and talked about. Attitudes toward money and its use come from many sources — "the way it was done at home," "the kind of person I like to think of myself as," reactions to fear, competition, insecurity. All play their role.

It is not easy to talk about money. A money economy can promote a compulsion to work which subordinates man to things. Issues of greed and competition arise as well as aggression and possessiveness. How the partners handle this defines the family values. The desire for money can take the place of other genuinely human needs. The apparent accumulation of wealth can impoverish human nature with too much value being placed on an industrious, cooly rational economic prosiac way of life, or there can be an ostrich like refusal to get involved with planning. "Why are we working and for what?"

Nowhere is it more difficult to talk about money than in planning for the future when one of the partners will be left a widow or widower. The sad reality is that three out of four American wives will become widows—a state for which there is no preparation. Knowing the insurance company statistics, a man can become defensive when the discussion of what will happen should his wife outlive him comes up. Many simply assume that things will work out and it is better to leave the matter unspoken rather than to tempt fate. *They are wrong!*

There are things that every wife must know that often only her husband can tell her—the precise value of their estate and the state and federal laws pertaining to it. No matter how little he has there should be a will for her protection and she should be aware of its terms. She should know of his participation in any company pension plan and if there are any alternatives in terms of a delayed or immediate payment so that she can select the one best for her. She must know what she is entitled to in the way of social security and veteran's or railroad pension benefits. There are often aspects and conditions of both pension and insurance plans that can come as an unpleasant surprise. The employment market for women in middle age is not high unless they have well developed skills. These realities must be taken into account.

Power and Control of One's Own Life

Because we identify ourselves with how we acquire and use money, it is also closely linked with our sense of personal power and therefore control over our lives. For most people, credit and debt directly oppose personal freedom. The head of a family may find himself locked into trying to meet all the payments with no freedom to improve his position with more training or to take time off to look for another job. His inner resentment may then be displaced unconsciously onto his partner and family.

In traditional marriage, money has been associated with the masculine role. Earning money gives one status. Society still places high value on a woman living her life through and around her husband's career or work. Her interests often narrow to house and children when she marries and the years go on. Her sense of self-confidence from being in touch with the outside world diminishes. Raising children, organizing domestic life and maintaining the family emotional equilibrium do not rank high in social value. In terms of emotional support and understanding, it occurs to few men to give what they get.

Women's liberation, in focusing attention on these injustices, has tended to offer women only role models of power, equality and success based on job opportunities and functions of men. An authentic model of what it is to be feminine, equal but not the same, with unique qualities and strengths in and out of family life—a whole person, is not yet visible to many women, nor to most men. Our entire society lacks a creative relationship to the feminine. Our system of monetary valuing is one of the factors which prevents this from emerging.

In every society there are tasks divided between men and women. Women are usually concerned with child care, collecting and producing certain agricultural products, preparing food, and care of the family dwelling. Men traditionally have taken care of such things as hunting, fishing, group defense and religion. Neither set of tasks is less important than the other. All are essential or survival of the group is threatened. Today, however, this functional division of labor has been disrupted for women. Women, whose role in frontier American society used to be vital to the family economy—gardening, canning fruit and vegetables, baking bread, milking cows, tending chickens, even making the clothing and bedding—now find themselves presiding over car pools and laborsaving devices. Any group, whose work role is undermined grows dissatisfied with itself and the society. The society, in turn, grows dissatisfied with the group. These social forces begin to evolve new work roles.

So far the trend has been increasing for women to enter the labor market to supplement family income in order to sustain a rising standard of living, i.e. to continue to buy the products of technology pushed by advertising. However, the job market, traditionally a male domain, has posed obstacles for women. It is not only that careers demanding full intellectual committment and years of specialized training are difficult for a woman to carry, the biological phases of her life and the child-bearing years divide her attention. But also, because many jobs, perhaps most, consist of drudgery with little meaning and dignity involved except as a means of keeping food on the table. Women, in pushing for equal rights to job opportunities may overlook a more basic issue — what are the appropriate and unique tasks of the feminine in this complex and rapidly changing society?

Only partners who basically feel themselves to be equal, can fully respect each other and women are increasingly pushing the limits of their roles to achieve this power of equality. The interim phase, however, has many stresses. There is some feeling that the baby may have been thrown out with the bath water as more married women give preference to work and career over household, as parental authority erodes, as the tendency grows to change the marital contract to an open or active marriage which expects less and less. There is a tendency to pledge as little as possible, "for as long as we are happy together." Marriage is viewed primarily for one's personal development rather than as a joint enterprise.

The feminine, in terms of both biological and cultural conditioning, has been concerned with nurturing and relatedness. Something is out of kilter with it in our culture. Large numbers of people complain of an inability to feel and a conviction of being unlovable. They feel apathetic, a lack of passion and a loss of the capacity to be intimately personal. With increasing possibilities for sexual gratification, the goal of having sex without any personal commitment, much less falling in love, is common.

Issues of power between men and women have been projected and displaced. It is difficult to admit we are motivated in our love by lust for power, anger and revenge. But these elements are present and we confront the dilemma of using them with awareness and responsibility. Love and hate in relationship are not polar opposites. They go together. (Apathy is the opposite of both.) In loving there is required a self-assertion, a capacity to stand on one's own feet in order to put oneself into the relationship. But assertion of one's own individuality always verges on the edge of exploitation of the partner for both man and woman. Yet without it there is no vital relationship or way of making certain one is valued.

Human consciousness works in polarities. The positive does not come out unless the negative does also. We fail each other when we try to hide this negative power drive, fail to confront it head on, deny it in ourselves and project it onto others or when we try to drug it with alcohol, work or other diversions. The furies in Greek literature were the spirits of anger, revenge and retaliation, the disturbers of sleep but they were always associated with issues of fate, guilt and personal responsibility. The necessity was then and is now to struggle with these issues to a new level of consciousness in order to integrate them and not to be overwhelmed. We each can know our own aggressive, cruel and hostile aspects, the things about ourselves that horrify us most.

Accepting that they *are* there can open the way for development of human understanding and compassion. The extravagant anger which many women are feeling and expressing today, the confusion and demand is still limiting, still dependent on and defined by that which it is protesting against. The deepening and widening of consciousness that we seek consists not in solution of these dilemmas but confronting them in such a way that we rise to a higher level of personal and interpersonal integration. The moral problem is to find our own conviction and at the same time to admit that there will always be an element of distortion and self aggrandizement in it.

Communication is *not* the important issue in itself. It is only a means. The need is for the partners to modify the way they define what they expect. They need to realign their ideas of self worth and to change their role relationships in order to reduce the ambiguities for each. The partners each need to increase the gratifications and sense of power-control over his/her own life that each gets from being married and carrying out the functions that he/she values. As this is done, society too will have to shift its orientations, for example, to really credit the complexity of the mothering function and provide for the development of the needed skills.

Sex and Affection

Emotional ties and the desire to be sexually involved with one's partner vary with one's sense of self-esteem. Affection and caring between partners is expressed in two ways—being responsive to each other and being responsible for the other (in the sense of wanting to take care of him or her). Responsiveness is a body state—the sudden surge of interest and attraction. Responsibility is invoked by the mind, an acknowledgement of obligation. Each partner says to the other in effect "I care very much about your feelings because your feelings affect mine."

Initially each partner expects to be faithful to the other simply because he/she wants to — if for no other reason than the feeling of being uniquely individual to one another. They each realize that if either seeks sexual satisfaction with other partners, the fewer satisfactions will they need from each other. The less they need, the easier to go their separate ways. Beyond all rationalizations, extramarital affairs demonstrate two things: firstly, that the partners have been incapable of meeting each other's basic physical and emotional needs, and secondly, that they did not consider each other unique and therefore irreplaceable as a source of satisfying pleasure.

The affirmation and acceptance of oneself as a sexual human being happens only in a mutually appreciated physical relationship. It exerts a powerful emotional effect on self-esteem. Every person hopes to find mirrored in the eyes of his/her partner an image of himself or herself as a sexually desirable person. In the intimacy of a sustained sexual relationship, few things matter more than to be seen as unique and desirable. To make a commitment to another person is an expression of loyalty. It also means trusting one's physical and emotional well-being to that partner. It involves an acceptance of vulnerability.

Making a commitment and becoming committed are two different matters. One can make a commitment to be personally loyal and to be a cooperative partner in maintaining a family — and yet *not* be committed in the sense of trusting the other with one's deepest feelings and becoming emotionally vulnerable.

Many people do not glimpse this distinction as they find themselves wrestling with the needs and problems of married life. They are obliged to set new priorities on making money, setting up a home and becoming established. Generally when couples discover they no longer feel like married lovers, they have begun to act more like business partners with specialized responsibilities. They slowly have become emotionally uncommitted and seem to be left only with formal obligations. This dis-involvement is experienced as each being less interested in the other. Each feels less cared for, less valued and less desired—which is one of the main reasons why sex grows unsatisfactory.

In this stage partners make little opportunity to spend time together and have little to say beyond discussing their separate obligations. So it is hardly surprising that sex, too, may begin to seem an obligation. At least to one of them at times, it seems an imposition.

Frequently, the relationship deteriorates from the couple's lack of a secure sexual bond to begin with. Insecurity in one or both partners may flow from negative sexual attitudes and early repressions. It may flow from unfortunate sexual experiences, or simply from lack of sexual information.

Howard and Roxanne are an example. In their early sexual encounters, Howard's inhibitions were not too apparent to either of them. They felt sufficient drive to get past inhibitions and both thought that with time, things would work out. This is frequently a correct assumption when the partners are aware of what it is to be a sexual person.

Howard, however, came from a family where intellect was everything and the body of interest only in that it supported the mind. He was seldom aware of sexuality sensed in spontaneous sexual impulses generated within the body, much less enjoying it as healthy and good. He had a habit of shallow breathing which effectively prevented buildup of excitement and tension which would require release. He felt uncomfortable in taking responsibility for actively reaching out and satisfying his sexual feelings. He unconsciously blocked pleasure from the total sensual experience for both Roxanne and himself.

The chief obstacle to sexual pleasure is fear—fear of being hurt, fear of being wrong, fear of being ridiculed— an almost endless list. Just as willingness to risk and become vulnerable to another human being brings one closer to that person, unwillingness to be vulnerable leads to self-protection, which leads to unwillingness to risk and to becoming uncommitted.

This reaction to fear, the closing off of risking often re-enacts a script that was written in childhood. When individuals encounter their first conflicts in marriage, they find it easy to react with deadened feelings. Just as they once did with their parents, they now react to their marriage partners by hiding behind defensive barriers. The partner in turn becomes guarded if not equally defensive. Howard, who had sensed the possibility of a different life with Roxanne, a deeply sensual woman, withdrew when he inwardly judged himself unable to meet what she *might* demand. With such a response, Roxanne felt not valued and was not willing to risk his further disinterest. They both were willing to stay invested in the marriage, but there was not the emotional commitment which would allow each to fully unfold emotionally.

Such a marriage can nevertheless be "successful." Their commitment is governed by reason and practical considerations rather than emotion and feelings are generally low keyed. The partners can respect one another and even share the kind of affection that reflects comfort with familiar things and persons, but there is no particular hunger to explore and enjoy the nature of their personalities, no sensing of possibilities beyond.

People often settle for this type of marriage. Although they married to feel close, neither finds this with the other. The man frequently feels more personally unique in his work and recreational relationships with other men, and the woman shifts her emotional investment to her children. Fidelity does not express their sexual commitment. It is rather the passive acceptance of a way of life which the husband and wife either do not wish to change or do not know how to change.

Masters and Johnson maintain that the ability of a man and woman to become sexually committed to one another stands or falls on their willingness to give and receive pleasure in all its forms. If a man and woman are committed to the enjoyment of their own sexual natures and to each other as sexual persons, intercourse allows them to express their feelings in whatever ways seem desirable at the moment, revealing themselves not only to each other but also to themselves. Responding to the urgencies of their own bodies as well as to the urgings of their partner, their actions embody their feelings, without requiring justification. There is no pressure to perform or pretend. When occasionally sex proves disappointing or unsatisfactory, they are secure in knowing there is always a tomorrow.

> Total commitment, in which all sense of obligation is linked to mutual feelings of loving concern, sustains a couple sexually over the years. In the beginning it frees them to explore the hidden dimensions of their sexual natures, playing with sex as pastime and passion, seeking the erotic pleasures that give life much of its meaning. Then, when carrying the inescapable burdens that come with a family and maturity, they can turn to each other for the physical comforting and emotional sustenance they need to withstand economic and social pressures that often threaten to drain life of all joy. Finally, in their later years, it is in the enduring satisfaction of their sexual and emotional bond that committed husbands and wives find reason enough to be glad that they still have another day together. (William H. Masters and Virginia E. Johnson, *The Pleasure Bond: A New Look at Sexuality and Commitment.* Boston: Little, Brown & Co., 1975, p. 268.)

Every individual evolves a unique set of needs that have to be met if satisfying sexual feelings are to result. These values influence all aspects, time, place, mood, words used, gestures, the thousand and one little signals that a man and woman send to one another with or without language. Each individual requires this to respond emotionally, to allow feelings to come to the surface. It also includes elements that permit the individual to be comfortable with those feelings. For instance, a man may have a desperate need to be held, to be touched and stroked, but when this happens, his full response may be blocked by guilt or embarrassment. Or a woman may know what would stimulate her but feels she cannot tell her partner to do it.

In countless marriages, conflicting feelings about intercourse on any given occasion are the rule rather than the exception and rarely are they easily resolved. Negative approaches to the conflict involve minimizing dissatisfaction, or becoming defensive or, worse yet, denying that any problem exists. Another ill-advised approach is to take the sexual problem out of context, viewing the physical aspects as skills to be mastered. This reduces sex to a compartmentalized act.

This is not to say that sexual awareness and sensitivity should not be cultivated as such. Sex manuals are seldom useful, but a book such as Jack Rosenberg's *Total Orgasm* teaches a process of body awareness of sexual feelings as they develop from within and allows an understanding of body blocks, and the ways one unconsciously prevents the full flow of his or her full feeling responsivity.

Sexual conflict is not a problem in need of solution; it is a situation that requires resolution. It requires that each partner be motivated to change and that each credit the other with good intentions, that their past discord need not repeat itself. Each must strive to be responsive to the other, not *responsible* for the other. Each accepts responsibility for his/her own sexual functioning and does not hold the other accountable for "making it happen." Then each must give up the "right-wrong" game—sometimes expressed in other words: should/shouldn't, free/uptight, healthy/unhealthy. Differences cannot be settled in terms of either/or. They can be negotiated, not in the sense of bargaining but as conciliation. Both have to change their habitual ways of interacting and success depends on how failure is handled—that occasional failures are not used against either partner. Very few couples start out perfectly matched in the strength of their sexual desires. For a compatible relationship, they have to reach a mutual understanding of their individual natures, and accept them for what they are. Each has to take into account that the other is not only fallible but also temperamental, and that they cannot and do not always act as they would like to. Apologies are O.K. after something has gone wrong. There are no shortcuts in achieving genuine intimacy. Trust and willingness to continue are the essence.

Children

Having a child does not improve a shaky marriage. A parent can believe that through his child he can experience the things he was denied or perhaps failed at as a child. He/she can believe that having a child will develop qualities in the other parent, for instance, a sense of responsibility. Children require a great deal of care and attention, which often conflicts with their parents' own needs and desires. Because parents can't easily admit their sense of deprivation and cannot feel guilty at having children, they sometimes end up blaming each other. The child's presence in a troubled marriage brings new problems.

Sometimes a child, or even an animal pet, can be used by one partner to divert and express the loving attention that the other partner longs for. Later as the children grow, it is not uncommon for one partner to use them to undermine the other's sense of authority and power. He/she manages this by unwittingly encouraging the children to break the rules established by the other when he/she is trying to be "in charge." For example, the father who slips his child a "treat" when the mother has made a "no eating before supper" rule. Or the mother who lets her son go for an overnight stay, after the father has indicated he wants the son to clean the garage. The most problematic action for one partner to undertake is to protect the child from the other. Too often a parent forgets that the child has a right to a separate relationship with each parent. In fact, this exists whether or not the other parent wishes it were different. The child negotiates and learns from each one of them aspects of life that the other cannot teach.

Jennie expressed this: "I spent my life protecting the boys from Jim, explaining each of them to the other. One day I heard them shouting at each other and I suddenly realized they were enjoying it. Jim is Ronnie's *father*. Ronnie knows him in a way that I can't. I can't protect him from having the father he has — and he doesn't want me to."

A most valuable aid to parenting today is P.E.T. (Parent Effectiveness Training) which teaches a method of active listening. This is available from some family agencies and in many adult education systems. The simple question "who owns the problem?" often removes the parents entirely from the issue.

Alcohol

In my experience there is seldom a marital therapy group in which alcohol does not figure as a problem for one or more couples. Most often it is the husband who admits he might be using alcohol to excess, but rationalizes it as a necessary adjunct to his work life. There are good resource books on the problems of the alcholic. What seems important to me is my observation that the drinking partner is always playing a "con game." In TA terms it is a con game from the Child ego state, which induces the other partner to come on as Critical Parent. The drinker produces all kinds of rationalizations, feels misunderstood and from this, justified in continuing his ways. The drinker does not take responsibility for the "setup" function of the behavior which effectively prevents not only intimacy, but also any real contact between the partners.

Ken and Laura are an example. Ken enjoyed his reputation as a hard-drinking Irishman even as a teenager. He was the middle child of seven and won attention only by being outstanding in everything he touched. Laura, his German war bride, was an only child raised by grandparents who treated her as a miniature adult and expected proper behavior from her on all occasions. Laura delighted in Ken's wild child aspect which she longed to express herself. After marriage, however, a pattern began. Ken, expected home at 6:00 p.m. would phone at 6:20 to say he was having a drink with some business friends and should be leaving in about another 20 minutes or so. He then might arrive home anywhere from an hour and a half to three hours later. When Laura objected, he maintained she was hassling him. She had to understand that business was business. Didn't she have any sense of humor? How in the world had he married such a killjoy. Buried under words, she would eventually give up and retreat feeling vaguely guilty at being so much like her Prussian grandparents. The weekend would come and another round of parties. Ken, socializing with his friends, scarcely noticed that Laura did not feel comfortable reaching out to people without his presence, and was totally unaware of her acute embarrassment when totally drunk, he either "passed out" or performed some prank.

Ken and Laura had to recognize the underlying needs in their own and the other's behavior. Ken had an almost insatiable hunger for affection and attention, which had not been met in his early life, and he also held an inner hopelessness about receiving it, along with resentment that it would not be given. Laura had never been able to be a child, spontaneous and free, longed for this but was frightened to let go, and reacted to this aspect in herself as to Ken's drinking with the Critical Parent state she had learned from her grandparents.

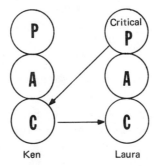

It seems that excessive misuse of alcohol is a choice when both partners are reluctant to face the deep dependency and needs they feel the other "should" meet for them. They structure a parent-child situation with intense, albeit negative, feelings toward one another. Only when their ambivalent feelings and the underlying needs are seen, can this be changed.

The best defense against the emotional impact of a partner's alcoholism is to gain knowledge and to work to achieve the emotional courage to put it into practice. Alcoholism has a tremendous emotional impact on the immediate family. The interaction may and often does become destructive rather than helpful. An essential first step is to recognize that one partner is *not* ever responsible for alcoholism in the other. Jennie and Jim both drink. Each blames the other for his/her drinking. Jim feels he needs some kind of an escape from coping with the accelerating demands of his job. "Jennie does not make it any easier with her erratic emotional demands, her depressions, her drinking to excess then using pills to reach a comatose state in which her life is endangered." Jennie drinks to forget her fear of what will happen to her if anything happens to Jim. "He doesn't take care of himself. He's killing himself working day and night and he plays as hard as he works. He doesn't expect to live past 50. I can't live with the worry of it." Each abets the other in avoiding real treatment, in taking the essential step—to stop drinking. "I'm not an alcoholic. I can go without a drink for weeks."

Neither can make the other take this first step. Each is responsible for himself alone.

Neither partner can treat the other. Because each partner, whether he/she drinks or not is emotionally troubled by the problem, each has to seek help for his own situation. The problems of alcohol do not lie in the bottle but in persons. Recovery, however, does not begin until the alcoholic is able to practice continued abstinence. No one can do for the alcoholic what must be done by the alcoholic. His/her choices and his/her actions are the only basis of permanent recovery. But giving up his/her control of the family is difficult. And how the alcoholic controls! He/she drinks again and again. The partner yells, screams, begs, pleads, threatens or withdraws into martyred silence. The partner *also* covers up, protects, and shields the alcoholic from the consequences of drinking.

The alcoholic continues the game with two weapons — one, the ability to arouse anger and provoke loss of temper. He projects onto the other his own self hatred and if the other responds, the alcoholic in his own mind feels justified in his past drinking and now has an additional excuse for further drink. The second weapon is his/her skill in arousing anxiety in the family. They feel compelled to do for the alcoholic that which only he should do, e.g., they cover for a bad check, make excuses so he won't be identified as drinking and lose his job, lose his license to drive, whatever. No one faces the reality of the situation and as the alcoholic's sense of failure and guilt increases, the family's hostility and condemnation does also. The alcoholic can never learn to solve his/her own problems in a responsible way if the anxiety of the partner compels the removal of the problem before he/she can be brought to face it and solve it or suffer the consequences. The partner and other family members need help in handling their own anxiety during this period — and to take a closer look at whatever their own "needs" might be which have been met by having the pain that living with an alcoholic entails. For example, maso-

chism is the need to suffer in order to find a sense of meaning in life.

Another "sick" need can be to dominate and control or
to have someone to punish. In other words, the place to begin to help an alcoholic recover is to begin with yourself.
Then you can work to help the partner to have a desire to
stop drinking and to accept help. Motivation has two aspects, discomfort and hope. The discomfort of drinking and
all its consequences has to become so painful in itself that
the alcoholic will look for escape from the intolerable pain
caused by his/her drinking. There can be no shielding from
this. Hope that things can be different can be found in the
fact that they have become different for thousands of re-
covered alcoholics and their families. The evidence can be
obtained along with the means through such associations as
Alcoholics Anonymous for the drinker, Al-Anon for the
partners of drinkers, Al-Ateen for the children. Other
effective types of help can be sought through local mental
health clinics, community alcoholism information centers
and some counselors and ministers with extensive experience
in this field.

In each of the foregoing problem areas, money, power,
sex, children and alcohol, conflicts arise, based on the different needs and understanding of the partners of how these
needs are to be met.

Suggested Exercises

MONEY: Think over the past week. What decisions about
money were made by you? By your partner? In which areas
did one partner's decisions have priority over the other? How
long ago was this priority agreed to and on what basis?

Try to remember exactly how the decision was reached. Is
the present allocation of decision-making realistic and using
each of your talents?

Before marriage you managed your money separately. When you married, how did you decide to merge your money? Did one assert control on the basis this was the way it had been done in his/her family? Did either have a different feeling and how was this handled? For example, a woman may regard her husband as a spendthrift but submerge this feeling because she thinks his self-esteem would be threatened and he would love her less if she were to insist on managing the money. But when tired of evading bill collectors she finally insists on taking over, the cost is a cold war of blame and guilt. Neither partner differentiates between their feelings of self worth and managing the finances. What feelings do you have about the decisions you have made? What feelings do you have about the way you handle differences between you and your partner? Think about a specific conflict. What are the values involved? What experiences led you to hold the values you do and how had your partner formed his/her values?

POWER: Ask your partner to share an experience with you. You are to reverse roles and take each other's place. Speak *as if you were your partner* and express "your" feelings about the power relationship between you and what is wrong with it. For instance, a wife *playing her husband* might say "I really get angry when you cut me off when I try to talk to you about budgeting. I feel discounted, like I don't matter at all." Express all your irritations, dislikes, annoyances, unhappinesses. Try to really feel as your partner, get into the experience of being him/her, seeing things from his point of view and expressing this viewpoint. Take at least 10 minutes to do this and then let your partner take your point of view. When you have finished, share what the experience of being your partner meant to you and what the experience of hearing your partner express your point of view meant to you.

When two people establish a relationship it is because each can gain something from the other. Take turns telling each other what it does *for* you to be in your relationship. Begin each sentence "By being your husband/wife I gain . . ." or something similar. Take about five minutes to do this. Now take a few minutes to share your experience in doing this. How did you feel and what did you become aware of?

Every relationship develops many unexpressed rules and assumptions about what is permitted, what is avoided, who does what, etc. Each person's role requires certain things and behaviors from the partner. Take turns telling each other what your own role in your relationship demands of your partner. Begin each sentence "In order for me to be a good wife/husband you must . . ." Develop all the details of what your roles demand of each other. Take about five minutes each to do this then share how you felt and what you became aware of about your relationship as you did this. See if you can think of any "ground rules" you missed. How might you want to change these?

SEX AND AFFECTION: Read each item in the list which follows and each partner can check whether he/she is 1) satisfied, 2) would like some improvement, or 3) feels this is an area which needs much more development between you.

	1. O.K.	2. Some improvement	3. Need to develop
I. *Love play and expression of affection*			
1. Showing tenderness, affection in everyday living (not just as a way of asking for intercourse)			
2. Giving daily consideration and understanding.			

3. Creating a romantic atmosphere — candlelight dinners, flowers, surprises.

4. Bathing, massaging and perfuming the body.

5. Having sufficient privacy together.

6. Loving stimulation of sensitive body areas.

7. Gentle, loving caressing of sex organs.

8. Strong, concentrated caressing and manipulation of sex organs.

9. New ideas for love play. (Suggest some.)

10. Sharing fantasies with each other.

11. Reading articles or books and/or discussing together ways to enhance and enrich love play.

12. Setting an atmosphere for loving and intercourse, experimenting with love play and intercourse at unusual hours — midsleep, early morning, before dinner, outdoors in the sun.

13. Planning weekends away together or . . . (suggest some others)

II. *Intercourse*

1. Sensitivity to each other's moods and feelings during intercourse.

2. More prolonged intercourse.

3. More or less (underline which) body movement during intercourse.

4. Achieving a satisfactory climax.

5. Frequency or number of times of intercourse.
   (Note desired frequency weekly____)

6. Having orgasm by other means:
   mouth-genital
   using hands
   mouth-breasts-hands-genital
   other:

7. Investigating other contraceptive methods.

8. Using different positions in intercourse.

9. Discussing the role of spiritual and different emotional elements in intercourse and sexual expression.

10. Reading together on different techniques of intercourse.

III. *After Intercourse*

1. Expressing love, tenderness and affection after intercourse.

2. Length of time spent together after intercourse.

3. Doing something for partner after intercourse. (Suggest some.)

4. Repeated intercourse following the first time.

5. Creating a different pattern— doing something different after intercourse.

CHILDREN: Review what you want of your child in relation to what kind of person you are around him/her. For example, you want him to be happy, is home a cheerful place to be? You want him to be creative, do you get excited about new things? You want him to learn, how many books did you read this past month, the past year? You want him to have ideals, how do you show yours and how do you tell him what you believe? Are you compassionate about the needs of people outside your family? Where do you experience differences with your partner on these values? How do you resolve them?

Can you as parents support one another with your children? Are your messages clear, given in such a way that they preserve the child's as well as the parent's self-respect? Is there a tendency to placate, to avoid issues, to blame, or to preach?

How do each of you tolerate feelings and ideas from your children which differ from your own? How do you decide who owns the problem, i.e., that it is an issue for the child to decide or that it is a family matter. How do you handle your anger? What are the specific issues that particularly trouble you with your children—physical behavior, dishonesty, rudeness, irresponsibility, jealousy, shyness, anxiety, aggressiveness, immaturity? How do these differ from your partner's issues? How do you support each other in coping and when do you decide you need additional help?

ALCOHOL: Read the following list. If you answer yes to any *one* of the questions, there is a definite warning that you may be an alcoholic. These questions are used by Johns Hopkins University Hospital, Baltimore, Maryland, in deciding whether or not a patient is an alcoholic. If you answer yes to any two, the chances are that you are an alcoholic. If you answer yes to three or more, you are definitely an alcoholic.

*Are You an Alcoholic?** To answer this question, ask yourself the following questions and answer them as honestly as you can.

	Yes	No
1 Do you lose time from work due to drinking?	☐	☐
2 Is drinking making your home life unhappy?	☐	☐
3 Do you drink because you are shy with other people?	☐	☐
4 Is drinking affecting your reputation?	☐	☐
5 Have you ever felt remorse after drinking?	☐	☐
6 Have you gotten into financial difficulties as a result of drinking?	☐	☐
7 Do you turn to lower companions and an inferior environment when drinking?	☐	☐
8 Does your drinking make you careless of your family's welfare?	☐	☐

*Alcoholics Anonymous, "Twenty Questions" leaflet. San Francisco: Inter-County Fellowship, Alcoholics Anonymous.

 9 Has your ambition decreased since drinking?   □ □
10 Do you crave a drink at a definite time daily?   □ □
11 Do you want a drink the next morning?   □ □
12 Does drinking cause you to have difficulty in sleeping?   □ □
13 Has your efficiency decreased since drinking?   □ □
14 Is drinking jeopardizing your job or business?   □ □
15 Do you drink to escape from worries or troubles?   □ □
16 Do you drink alone?   □ □
17 Have you ever had a complete loss of memory as a result
    of drinking?   □ □
18 Has your physician ever treated you for drinking?   □ □
19 Do you drink to build up your self-confidence?   □ □
20 Have you ever been to a hospital or institution on account
    of drinking?   □ □

The family's best resource against the emotional impact of alcoholism is gaining knowledge and the emotional maturity and courage to put it into effect. The partner of the alcoholic may need more assistance and counseling than the alcoholic if an effective recovery program is to take place. For example, the partner can find himself/herself blamed for everything that is wrong. This may reach the point where they may fear this is true. What needs to happen is a treatment program that involves everyone who is effected by the problem. Alcoholics Anonymous is probably the best known group program for such treatment. Al-Anon and Ala-teen are the adjunct groups for the support needed by the partner and the children of the alcoholic. You can learn more about treatment programs by contacting your local AA association or your community mental health association.

Chapter V

Problem Solving

Communication and Reconnecting

A quarter of a century ago, when I trained as a young social worker, the essential skill we were taught was listening. It wasn't easy to learn. What we were listening for were the feelings behind the words being said. We learned how our own feelings colored what we heard, how they screened out parts of the other person's message. We learned that if we formed opinions, judgments too soon, or thought we knew what the other person was getting at before he/she fully explored his/her problems — we were usually off track, filling in from our own background something that wasn't necessarily so for the other person. We had to learn to observe body language and to listen to the tone of voice which indicated how the message was to be understood. We learned that the feelings being voiced often covered more painful hidden feelings. And finally we had to learn that we often could not use our new knowledge directly because the person himself might not want to own his under-feelings until he trusted our relationship.

Today, much of what I do is still in listening and teaching my clients and students to listen, to be aware of what they themselves, as well as the other person is saying. And the same rule applies: you have to relate to the feelings before you can understand the facts.

We have better ways of teaching now. Over the years a body of knowledge about communication has built up and the suggestions that follow cover some of the essential points applied to marital problem solving. This largely deals with the verbal level. To understand the nonverbal, a session with videotape is invaluable and this is used in marriage therapy to pay attention to posture, gestures, facial expression, the level and tone of voice, repetitious behaviors— foot tapping, arm crossing, turning away, inappropriate laughter—that condition the other to respond in certain ways. We cannot easily cover these aspects in a book however so the next best substitute might be for you to use an inexpensive cassette tape recorder while you discuss with your partner some issue of conflict between you.

When you replay the tape, listen to your voice tone. Does it match what you were saying? What you were feeling? Be gentle in your observations. Don't judge yourself as "doing it wrong," just be aware as you can in an impartial way. Listen to the way you structure your messages. Are you mostly sending "you" messages, telling the other how he/she should feel, act or think? Are you analyzing or evaluating your partner's personality or behavior? Even when you don't intend it, "you . . ." messages have a way of coming over as parental, or judgmental. They are not straight and equal. They put distance between you and usually elicit a defensive, if not an adversary reaction from your partner. Listen to your messages that start with "I am . . .," "I think . . ." or "I feel . . ." Do you hear the difference? You are saying something about you, how it is with you, where your concerns are—and you can probably pick up from the tape that your partner hears these messages more clearly. A defensive listener tends to close up and pay attention only to the threat aspects. When there is no need to defend, there is more openness and more information gets through.

Now you may want to try the conversation again. This time say "I" and "me" whenever you can. Express *yourself* and avoid talking about your partner. Avoid the temptation to take responsibility for your partner through interpreting his/her behavior or by telling him/her what you think his/her problem is. Concentrate on expressing your own feelings as they arise in the dialogue—fear, resentment, appreciation, anxiety. Ask and state what you want. Don't expect your partner to know intuitively what you feel or need. This matter of *expressing* feelings has to be learned carefully. You probably have many ways of indirectly *showing* feelings. For instance, icy silence for many people is a way of showing anger but expressing it is another matter. You own your feeling by saying *what* it is, *how* it feels and *what* the situation is that has produced it. The more conscious you can be of your feelings as you actually experience them in your body, the more accurate will be your expression. For instance, fear is often felt as a tightening of the upper chest and throat or as a dryness in the mouth. We have lots of phrases in English that tell us where feelings are felt: "He was bellyaching about his job." "It makes me want to throw up." "She's a pain in the neck." "Get off my back." "My heart was in my throat." "It makes my blood boil." "My heart sank to the pit of my stomach." Pay attention to your own bodily sensations, headaches, tightness in the arms and legs, sexual excitement, tense muscles to know better when you are feeling bored, enthused, resentful, disgusted. These sensations often need to be recognized and expressed.

The most helpful rule I know is to watch out for the phrase "feel that . . ." You can start a sentence "I feel . . . ," but if you tack on the word "that," what follows is not a *feeling* at all but a judging statement usually directed at the other person.

This is probably enough to practice for one session, or maybe even for many. It takes time to modify patterns of expression but taking responsibility for expressing your own feelings, your own wants, your own needs is the crucial first step.

The second step is to pay attention to the content — what you are saying. To really resolve an issue, you have to be willing to give up the past and stick to the present here and now situation with specific events, feelings and people involved, and to be specific about what you want. Generalizing words "always," "never" only add a buzz of confusion, a fog in which no issue can be grappled. When you say, "we never go any place anymore," are you saying you would like to spend more time with your partner? Are there things that you used to enjoy doing together that you would like to do again? Are you wanting him/her to think up new things for you to do, or would you like to do something and you think he/she would not be interested?

When you find the basic issue between you, state it and STOP. Wait for your partner's response. Do not bury your statement with words. If you have the real issue, the bare statement will be direct and powerful. Each time you do this, work toward finishing it between you, so that you both know and acknowledge that this issue can be closed and is finished.

Neither will add it to a list of grievances against the other, a "gunnysack" of proof that the other does not care.

When drawing your partner into discussion, watch the kinds of questions you ask. Are they really questions or your opinion masked as a question. For instance, "Don't you think she is too young to stay out this late?" When you catch yourself asking one of these non-questions, turn it into a statement, i.e., "I think that she is too young to stay out this late," to check if this is what you are in fact saying. Then stand behind it. What do you want to do about it?

Avoid "why" questions and replace them with "what" and "how" if you want to get something settled. "Why" seems to lead to analyzing and rationalizing — to being a philosophizer rather than an engineer who comes up with a workable solution. Avoid leading questions: "Did that make you feel angry?" Open-ended questions: "How did you feel about it?" Allow your partner to respond in a freer, more spontaneous way.

Be willing to call a halt when you are just not "getting through to one another." Anyone can have a bad day. When you find this happening, acknowledge it and ask your partner to set a specific time with you when you can continue. The complete process of communication involves three steps — sending a message, acknowledging receipt and responding. Both of you have to be ready to work at this.

People are often frightened of their angry feelings, afraid to let them out because they might be too strong, too ugly. In childhood, they may have witnessed destructive anger that seemed out of control or they may have been hurt physically or emotionally by a sadistic violent parent. They might fear their own anger will drive the partner away, or there might be some cost to pay for expressing it that the person feels he/she cannot handle. One might appear ridiculous or foolish — particularly, if the other person seems to have a better way with words or logic.

Sometimes anger builds up when one person feels obliged to give to the other. Nine times out of ten he/she gives because it feels right and expresses love. The tenth time he might give feeling "I can't *not* give, ever" and he resents it. Resentment is an uncomfortable feeling to own. When it is expressed you are directly in touch with what you want because you can always change a statement of resentment into a demand. "I resent being left with all the cleanup after we entertain" translates into "I want you to help me clean up." If you are unwilling to make your wish explicit, you must question how you are using your resentment, and why. It is important to let go of hidden anger, to unblock the life in your relationship — and incidentally in your own body. Unexpressed anger works its way through high blood pressure, ulcers, tension headaches and numerous other physical symptoms. When you can express anger NOW as you are feeling it, you won't distort it and it won't destroy you.

In addition to fears, people have a lot of rationalizations to help them block anger. The "debt of gratitude" is the commonest. "How can I possibly get angry at her after all she has done for me." Some people genuinely believe anger is destructive because they have no knowledge of healthy anger. If you can't express anger, however, you also block your self-assertion and your ability to protect and take care of yourself.

George Bach and his associates in "Fair Fight Training" have developed two "safe" methods for identifying and expressing anger. The first ("VESUVIUS") simply vents the anger, allows it to be expressed without evaluation, criticism or action consequence. The second ("HAIRCUT") embodies all the principles of good communication and is worth practice.

A "Vesuvius" is the full emotional expression of feelings that can no longer be bottled up. These feelings may stem from many sources: pressures at work, conflicts with the children, your partner, the state of the world, the transit system, your car battery going dead because you left the lights on, whatever. The feelings are there and they push to be expressed. Instead of looking for something to get mad about and then "dumping" the angry, frustrated feelings as you may have done in the past, you instead admit to your partner that you are really feeling pressure and you need to get these feelings out. You know some of them will sound unreasonable and you are not asking for a response, just to be listened to so you can clear your system. Ask for a specific amount of time: "I think I need five minutes." Your partner can agree with the understanding that he/she simply is your audience.

When you are doing this for your partner, be a good audience, pay attention and encourage the full expression. It may turn into a comedy and you can applaud the style and vigor of your partner's performance. Whatever happens, the most important thing for you is to listen, to hear, NEVER to moralize, analyze, point out other approaches to problems, give advice. No, just listen, know and appreciate that these are the feelings your partner is struggling with. After the heat of feelings have been expressed, you may want to ask if the other wants to discuss some aspect further but this is not necessary.

The second device for expressing anger is used when the anger is specifically directed toward your spouse. It is called a "haircut." Here you pick some issue that you have quite a bit of feeling about and negotiate: "I am angry. I want you to understand what and how I am feeling about this situation. I want to give you a haircut and I want two minutes to do it in." You can ask for any length of time but it is amazing how much can be said in as little as a half minute and it rarely takes more than two minutes to state your point of view.

Your partner now has the option of agreeing or of stating a reason for refusing this particular time and setting another, e.g., "Honey, I am willing to hear your anger but can you wait until I have gotten this work out of the way? How about in a half hour?"

You sit facing your partner, knee to knee and when you are ready, keep track of the time and begin. You have the full time you negotiated for and your partner makes no response until this is up. If you reach the end of the time period and do not seem to have finished, your partner says: "the two minutes are up, do you need more time?" and you decide if you need a few more seconds to finish. When you do feel finished, your partner is to state back to you what he/she heard you say. He/she does this without editorializing, judging or interpreting. What you are interested in is that your message is accurately understood, *not that it is answered or agreed with*. If the message is not restated as you intended to send it, say so and restate this portion. Your partner then says "you are saying . . ." and if you experience that your partner has in fact stated your message correctly, you reach over and with a kiss, a pat or some other gesture, express your appreciation that your partner has made this effort to hear you exactly. Your partner may have another point of view, however, and some other feelings to be expressed, so in turn can negotiate for time to give you a haircut. The same procedure is followed: a timed statement, exact restatement and reward.

This exercise contains the essence of clear communication used in business, the military and in interpersonal problem solving. The message is sent. A signal is sent that it has been received and then a response is made. So much "bugging," "nagging," so much saying the same thing in the same way over and over again can be eliminated in this way when the partner can be sure that he/she has really been heard.

It may seem awkward to do this with every issue of conflict but when it is important to you that the other hear what you are saying or feeling, this will allow you to know that you have been heard. A side effect of practicing it a few times will be that you gain skill in giving feedback which can be used in many situations other than with your partner. Feedback is the process of observing behavior and describing back what you observe without adding judgments and interpretations. Eliminating your own subjective interpretations will allow you to see and hear a wider range of data. As you develop skill in repeating precisely and accurately, you will also be able to listen more closely to yourself and be aware of all of your complex responses.

A Different Point of View

One of the most baffling impasses in marriage seems to be the situation in which each partner, in the eyes of the other, is just not in touch with the *reality* of the situation. Moreover, he/she seems determined to hold onto his/her point of view no matter how carefully and with what masses of evidence one attempts to persuade him of the truth of the matter. Nothing short of sheer perversity would seem to account for it.

Jung's theory of personality types provides a slender bridge across this chasm of mutual incomprehension. People frequently really do each look out on a different scene and form judgments about it based on different sets of "obvious" data. Personality type develops from certain basic differences in interest and attention in the child. These interests start as inborn tendencies, grow into a habit of mind and can evolve into a highly differentiated skill, one of the four psychological functions—thinking, feeling, sense-perception or intuition.

You develop skill in *perception* primarily through detailed sensory data, being in touch with the facts, or through intuition, an overall sensing of the pattern of things or events. And you reach skill in *judging* either through thinking, impersonally weighing and analyzing cause and effect, discriminating between true and false, or through feeling. A feeling judgment is rooted in personal evaluation, the situation "feels right" or something "feels missing." Other persons' feelings weigh in the valuation as well as one's own.

The way you perceive and the way you judge determines your type. An additional dimension to this is whether you customarily focus on taking action in the outer world of people and things—in which case you are an extrovert—or whether you prefer to attend to the inner world of ideas and to reflect. Then you are an introvert. Both extroverts and introverts are indispensibly useful in this world but each needs some supplementary skill in the other direction.

Within these six possibilities there are endless possible combinations for, while there is a strong tendency to have one well developed favorite function, we have the other traits in varying degrees.

For example, the following chart outlines the characteristics of four types of people based on their customary

Person perceives:	Sensory Data Primarily		Intuitive Patterns	
His attention focus is on:	Facts approached with Impersonal Analysis	Facts approached with Personal Warmth	Possibilities approached with Impersonal analysis	Possibilities approached with Personal Warmth
His most skilled functions are:	Sense perception and Thinking	Sense perception and Feeling	Intuition and Thinking	Intuition and Feeling
Resulting traits:	Practical and Matter of Fact	Sociable and Friendly	Intellectually ingenious	Enthusiastic and insightful

ways of perceiving. Roughly 3 out of 4 people show more interest in sensory perception than intuition. They concentrate on existing facts and the evidence of their five senses. However, one out of every four, the intuitive, may be more attentive to the link between something seen and something not yet thought of. His/her attention focuses habitually on possibilities, and he/she may totally overlook what his/her partner considers "plain as the nose on your face."

The chart indicates that these different combinations produce different traits. In marital problems, we get into difficulty when two opposite types cannot understand the other's point of view.

For example, Paula is an introverted thinking type. Her husband, Dan, is extroverted and feeling. The secondary function for each of them is intuition. Paula, an attractive redhead from New England, studied engineering, then gave up a promising career to marry Dan, a lawyer. He preferred to practice in a semirural setting where the demand for lady engineers was not high. Paula enjoyed being a mother and found satisfying ways of being involved in community affairs, so most of the time she did not regret her lost career. However, as the children grew and required less of her time, she and Dan increasingly found themselves at loggerheads. Finally at a point of crisis they sought therapy. The crux for each of them was that they defined each and every situation differently.

Simple things like taking an auto trip were impossible. Dan liked the adventure of striking out into the unknown, refused to ask directions and only briefly consulted a map, preferring to trust his well-developed sense of direction and feel for the country. Paula, on the other hand, was invariably tense and miserable, feeling sure they were lost — as, in fact, they had been a few times in the past (times remembered as adventure by Dan and as harrowing escapes by Paula). As the day wore on, she would insist they stop, consult gas station attendants, grocery clerks, anyone in sight and with map in hand dispute the relative advantages of alternative routes. Dan, feeling his judgment was being attacked, would sit in stony silence in the car, until the fifth or sixth such stop for another consultation—then he would explode. Another vacation ruined.

Both enjoyed sports and games, but Paula played to win, while Dan was a shade more interested in the people than the game. Both were competent and competitive bridge players and enjoyed playing as partners. However, when their club took in some new members and Dan arranged the game nights, Paula refused to be teamed with beginners as it seemed a waste of her time. Dan expostulated with her but she said he "needed" to please everybody and that was not her problem.

The final straw was a fishing trip which Dan had prepared for months. Paula watched him read up on the traits of salmon, sort through fishing gear and discuss the strategy of fishing salmon with their son. She knew how much he was looking forward to the trip and she truly wanted him to thoroughly enjoy himself. She went along only because she knew he liked an audience. The day arrived. He invited an extra friend. They reached the water as a storm was rising. Dan took charge of the boat, as no one else had the skill, and turned his fishing gear over to Paula. She was seasick and hated the whole day. Dan claimed to have had a great time and she refused to believe him. His friend who had not even been interested had caught several fish; Dan had caught none after all that preparation and was stuck with the boat—how could he possibly have had a great time? Dan was furious with her analysis. Now she was even trying to tell him what he *felt! He* knew what he was feeling and he was *not* feeling as she thought he should feel.

Note that these two people genuinely care for each other and want the other to share in his/her interests, BUT each thinks the other should think and feel as he/she thinks and feels about a given situation. In fact, in each situation, each partner was behaving true to type in the best way he/she knew how to function.

Paula, as an introverted thinker, used her thinking to analyze situations but was not attempting to run them. She was always interested in identifying the underlying principles, the ideas and facts rather than the situations and people involved. All her life she had had the ability to become totally involved in anything she turned her mind to and was markedly independent of any external circumstances. She was decided and sure in all her ideas, and when Dan did not see the situations in the same light she did, or appeared to describe them inconsistently, she felt he was undermining her sanity, for surely what was so, was so. What she did not realize was that her concern always to state the *exact* truth often had a devastating impact on the people around her. For her own sense of security she needed to have things like road routes defined with few possibilities for error. Not to do this placed her in great tension, which Dan could not comprehend from his own nature. Her refusal to play bridge with beginners was again from an impersonal analysis of her enjoyment being related to skill more than to the people involved. She had no dislike for the people, why should they feel offended. It was similarly incomprehensible to her that Dan could have an alternative source of enjoyment when he had so obviously been investing in the fishing.

Dan, on the other hand, although highly skilled and competent in many areas, as a feeling extrovert was *chiefly* concerned with people. He was friendly, tactful, sympathetic and always able to tune into where other people were feeling. He enjoyed other people's good feelings toward him and was bothered when he sensed any indifference. One of his wife's complaints was that he would never think of asking his secretary to do anything extra and so was frequently late for dinner, finishing up office matters that others could have done for him. He had come from a family where no one asked anyone else to do anything unless he/she was fairly sure the other was willing. He had no memory of family conflicts and so tended to think the fault today was surely with Paula rather than himself. What he did not realize was how much he viewed Paula as an extension of himself and assumed she would be willing to go along with whatever inconvenience he, himself, would be willing to endure. His preference not to admit disagreeable facts led him to ignore Paula's analyses, which she would continue to restate in her clear staccato New England voice which, like sandpaper, finally ground him down.

Each had to realize that the other was operating within a completely different frame of reference which represented not only different value judgments but also different needs. Paula needed the security of a rational and known framework. She could then be her full, free self, able to enjoy Dan and whatever action was going on. Dan needed to be with people who appreciated him and he wanted Paula to approve and applaud his very real skills instead of always attending to what was wrong or missing.

Each had to recognize how he/she needed the other. Paula genuinely liked people, but was often unaware of her impact on them. Dan could help her to anticipate this and forecast how others would feel about her plans. He also had the ability to reach her enthusiasm and to make bridges for her with people she wanted to reach. Finally, he was able to truly appreciate her particular uniqueness. She was much like the child in the story about the emperor who had no clothes. She always stated the exact truth as she saw it. Few people have that kind of courage.

Dan, on the other hand, needed her to talk over his plans, to analyze and find flaws in advance, to help him weigh the evidence. This was O.K. with him when he finally realized she did *not* insist he do things her way, only that he indicate that he really heard her point of view; then he could make his own decisions. He had not been giving her any indications that he heard and understood her because this was mixed up in his mind with control.

He needed her help in standing firm and in being consistent when he had to face the fact that other people might not always feel good about decisions he had to make.

The foregoing example has illustrated the conflicts and mutual usefulness of the thinking type and the feeling type of personality. The other pair of opposites are intuition and sense perception. They too, need each other. The intuitive needs a sense perceptive friend to bring up pertinent facts and remember things that didn't seem relevant at the time they happened, to read over a contract, to proofread papers, to catch details and to have patience. The sense perceptive person needs the intuitive to supply originality, to deal with complexity and many imponderables, to spark things that seem impossible, to challenge tradition and sometimes just to explain what another intuitive is talking about.

You might think about your recurrent conflicts with your partner in this light. Can you identify where you might be viewing different aspects of the same facts and with different values of judgment? If so, you may have strengths for each other that you have not realized.

Resources in Your Marriage

The problems specific to marriage stem from the clash between your individual wishes and the limitations and restrictions of your freedom that you accept in order to sustain an ongoing committed relationship. The resources specific to marriage are similarly related to the committed relationship.

A marriage commitment, regardless of how it is worded, still involves undertaking some jointly shared tasks, making a home together, sharing an exclusive sexual bond whether "richer or poorer, in sickness or in health," and most of us at least *hope* that it will endure until "death do us part." The special strengths in marriage come from these realities. Each of you knows the other, at some point, cared enough to choose to make this commitment. The jointly shared tasks in making a home together and the married sexual bond have built up a shared multifaceted knowing of one another without illusions. Each is familiar, has "depth" in the eyes of the other that casual knowing never gives. When the marriage has lasted over a number of years, there have been enough crises shared, enough joys, enough disappointments that each has been able to risk feeling the range of his/her deeper feelings and has tested the other's response and degree of acceptance of all aspects of himself/herself. You each know yourself more fully as a result of your partner knowing you because identity is partly built on the perception of other persons responding to one's behavior. In marriage you probably have shown a wider range of behaviors than in any other relationship. You also have experienced your partner in this complex way.

Although, in times of crisis, you tend to see your differences in a heightened way, you actually have strong undercurrent bonds based in this familiarity which you may underestimate. The familiar and the known, even the problematic familiar and known, offers a certain sense of security. When you have gone through difficult times together, you have an experienced knowing that these times can be survived because you have done so. When you are currently focusing on what is lacking and less than satisfactory, your memories of love shared, of tenderness given and received, of shared pleasure in communicating the love between you grows dim. Finding some way to get past your defensive hurt and anger, some way to open up to these memories from your positions of "righteous indignation" is an important first step in taking a realistic look at what needs to be either rebuilt, strengthened or changed in your marriage — and what you have to build with and on.

First Steps in Reconstructing a Relationship

Backing away from a "Mexican Standoff" (combatants facing each other, guns drawn, neither wanting to fire the deadly shot yet neither wanting to lose face and drop the gun) takes courage. It involves the risk of going more than half way and not being met by an equal response. You take a chance in acknowledging the issue is not clear cut "I'm right. You're wrong." But rather "I'm *not* totally responsible for this but I know that I have had something to do with making things as bad as they are between us." Your partner *may* use your admission against you and may block your assertion that you are both involved. That *is* a risk.

"On the other hand, it is not much of a life living a cold war. So much energy gets used up. So many resources that could be channeled elsewhere. If I need to prove to you how wrong you are, I have to watch every minute and collect the evidence. And tell it over and over to myself so I won't forget it. I have to 'keep my steam up' so I can tell it to you with appropriate energy so it will make an impression. I have to define myself as a martyr (and a bit of a dummy) for putting up with such a situation. I have no time left over for thinking of what I like to do, having fun or inventing ways to make my life fuller. War costs a lot. Of course it keeps me busy if I can't face the thought of having all that time and energy to use up elsewhere. Making and storing ammunition gives full-time employment so I may hardly notice the cost — the diminishing quality of every other aspect of my life."

The very first step in reconstructing a relationship is something like the foregoing meditation. You have to recognize that you are involved in an interaction which for all its secondary gains in structuring your time and giving you a feeling of being "right" nonetheless does not make you feel very good and certainly not happy. Then you must think of the costs. And think also of what else you might do with your time and energy — possibly even with your partner.

Suggested Exercises

Take a current issue between you and your partner. What is your partner's point of view and what is your own? What is the central point of conflict? Is one trying to influence the other to do, be, or accept something? Do you object to *what* is at issue or *how* the other is attempting to influence you? Does the problem "belong" to one of you more than the other? Each of you write down, now, all of the things, advantages you would gain if your partner were to capitulate "You are right about this matter. I have come to agree with you." How would you feel? How would you feel about him/her? Imagine in as much detail as possible exactly what would change. What would you do differently and what would your partner do differently? What do you imagine the long term consequences would be?

Take a second sheet of paper and now envision exactly what the consequences would be if *you* were to go to your partner and say "You are right about this matter. I have come to agree with your point of view." How would you feel? What would you lose? How would your partner react? What is the worst possibility that could result? What do you imagine the long-term consequences to be? How would you behave differently? How would your partner behave differently? Imagine this as vividly as possible.

Now imagine yourself 15 years from now. What are the circumstances of your life? Who is around? Taking the viewpoint of the older "you," imagine an encounter with your younger self. Write out the advice you would give this person on the problem he/she is facing. Take a few minutes now to share with your partner what you have discovered.

Another exercise to explore your personal investment in playing the "right-wrong" game is done alone when you have time to put yourself into a state of relaxation for remembering. This is done in a quiet place where you will not be interrupted for a half hour or so. You lie on the floor facing up. If you want to cushion your head, you may although this is usually not necessary. Let go as much of the tension as possible in your body, then simply pay attention to your breathing. It may help to envision a balloon in your belly which inflates as you inhale and shrinks as you exhale. Otherwise you may just intone a sound or a single word—

"om" or "one" with each exhalation. After you have done this with eyes closed, 15--20 times, imagine that you are watching an inner movie screen and go back in time to an incident when you clearly felt that you were right and some other person did not see this. Remember exactly how you felt about yourself, the other person and what efforts you made to be understood. Now select another memory, this time when you felt in the wrong. Remember how you felt and what the circumstances were. Now go to an earlier time when you were "in the right" and judged to be "in the wrong." Review it for similarities of feeling and the things you attempted. Then go back to an earlier time when you felt "wrong." Continue this as far back as you can remember. When you have finished open your eyes and take a minute or so to look at your surroundings and bring yourself back to the "here and now" before you move. Then take your paper and write fully whatever occurs to you about how this issue of being right or being wrong affects your life.

Having decided that you want to reconstruct the relationship with your partner, how do you move? What do you say? Think back over past misunderstandings, what worked and made it feel o.k.? What really was not satisfactory and left a residual resentment? Is there any thing you admire, can accept or affirm in your partner's position? Is there any way you can both "win"?

Chapter VI

What's Right with Marriage

Ordinary consciousness has one peculiar characteristic. It tends to focus more on what is going wrong than what is going right. But, paradoxically, push and strain is part of what is *right* about marriage. It is not all that is right, of course. Marriage more than any other human relationship has the resources to develop your wholeness as a human being.

Some of the young people today who seem vehemently against marriage, are actually struggling to find new attitudes to match new social realities. Accomplishment of this aim will necessarily involve vast changes in their marriage process and the ways in which they see themselves. The struggle is one intrinsic to the growth of consciousness.

Development of you as a person and for you in your marriage does not mean you must successfully resolve all the differences between you and your partner. It does not even mean that you internally resolve your own problems. You become most fully yourself through the process of coping with an ever increasing depth of complex problems.

Most people assume that while children grow and change, adults only age. *Not so*. While children mark the passing years with their body changes, adults change principally in their minds. This process of change means coming

94

to new beliefs about yourself and the world. Beliefs are more felt than thought yet you must think about them so your experiences can modify them. The process of self-confrontation involves thinking honestly about what you really feel and what you are experiencing.

Your process of self formation continues throughout each decade of your life. Recently, Roger Gould, a psychoanalyst at UCLA, studied the phases of adult life with 524 men and women to probe just how it is that adults grow up. His major finding was that as you age, you tend to become more tolerant of yourself, more appreciative of the complexity of the surrounding world and more aware of self complexity. However, many things can divert, slow down or block that process.

In marriage, goals are only possible in relation to the development of two persons. Each of you has to understand what he/she is trying to get out of the marriage; what he/she is trying to do with his/her life in the marriage and how these meanings fit together in each phase of life as you live it together.

Adult Phases of Development and Their Impact on Marriage

The following sequence seems to be true for the majority of people. In each decade as the individual develops, he/she experiences corresponding possibilities and stresses in his/her marriage which forces him/her to grow further. The precise ages at which changes occur in your own life may differ according to the age you were when you married and to the personality type differences which we looked at in the last chapter. For now, we will assume you are typical.

Basically, if you married as an adolescent, some wish to escape from your parents' dominance may have influenced your decision. You also had to struggle with various feelings of anxiety and excitement in preparing to leave the family. In the next few years as your partner became more familiar and friends substituted for family, you felt more independent. The younger marriage, whether in adolescence or the early twenties, is often the first close relationship for both partners. The only life you know apart from the family in which you grew up is the one you yourselves build. Your love for one another, based on a shared identity, tends to make you feel you are meant for each other and that you understand each other, often without words. Each of you may be somewhat unclear where he/she begins and the other leaves off. You see in the other aspects of yourself which do not necessarily accord with the facts. This can give each of you a false sense of security. Life will challenge your assumptions, however, and as a couple you will replace them with more valid judgments as you go on.

New external problems keep younger married partners very much occupied. Making a home, providing an income sufficient for increasing needs, building up a social life takes your time and energy. When babies arrive, little leisure remains to become aware of the more subtle aspects of life. The problem of your own psychological "fit" and relatedness often will not intrude itself until middle age when the children are finally on their own and you have develolped a more secure financial position. Then each of you must work to find within yourself the qualities you have felt your partner to be carrying for so long. This is a typical point of crisis.

In your twenties, however, you are still coming into your own place in the world. In most instances you are more open to new ideas, less repressive than at any other period in life. It is a time to love; it is a time to build for the future, both personally and in your work. You concentrate your energies and willpower on becoming competent in the real world and with increasing self-reliance there is less use of friends as substitute family.

Each partner now is more likely to have well organized opinions on politics, religion, business, society and all other matters of general interest. If you are to get along together harmoniously, you must form a relationship that will leave you free to hold your individual opinions, based on your differences as much as your agreements. It is important that you talk out ramifications of your relations—finances, privacy needs for time apart, space and quiet, the right to see your friends alone, the obligations to unify your personal habits. Both of you may be completely unaware of unvoiced assumptions which can complicate matters. As a rule the man has one set of assumptions, the woman, another.

Take for instance, the matter of money. Ben and Sheila agree that Sheila will continue her job and their incomes be shared. When they decide to have a child "before Sheila gets too old," Ben realizes that he has to support his wife at least for a time. But now, far from acting on any liberal or modern theory of sharing alike, he falls back on an old model and does as his father and grandfather did before him. He supplies his wife with housekeeping money only. His assumptions about the obligations of marriage differ considerably from hers.

As with money, there are many other issues which you have to spell out with each other. "Cabin fever" is an old-fashioned term which covers the problems that come from a sense of suffocation with too much closeness. Sooner or later in marriage one or both of you realize that change in the relationship is taking place. You were probably not fully mature when you married, far from being your completed selves. The period preceding marriage has unvoiced assumptions anticipating the ones you form in marriage and at least a few romantic illusions. With that background, inevitably the marriage must change. It cannot stay where it is. To know this is to know that it is not a problem but rather a process of growth. It challenges you to be more real and allows the gradual unfolding of each partner's potentialities. These develop in unexpected ways. You experiment and discover the paradoxes in your experiences. For instance, letting go of blocked anger regarding money or lack of privacy may sometimes be the key to releasing your aliveness and creativity in finding new solutions. You find also, it doesn't destroy your love.

Experiencing and questioning seems to predominate in

your early thirties when your self-assurance about what you are doing (and why) often wavers. It is an interesting and active time but marriage absorbs and reflects many of its stresses and strains. There is often less satisfaction with the marriage relationship as such. On the other hand if you have children, they are increasingly important to you in these years. Children are a bond with your partner but often they also can serve to evade direct contact with each other. This would necessitate your taking a step toward resolving your differences. You would become more conscious of the implicit demands you make that your partner do for you. You are often preoccupied with not making or having enough money to do what you want and you want to blame the other for not providing or for mismanaging. Or you may feel the other person blames you for mismanaging or not providing.

In this phase of your life, questions are again pushing at you from inside about your meaning and purpose in life. You may be aware once more of social concerns and strivings that you had let go. What you are uncomfortable in facing in yourself may get displaced in impatience with your husband/your wife. It is important to understand how normal and valuable these dissatisfactions are in pushing out your own growing edge. The temptation is to think that someone else could understand you better without recognizing that you are struggling to define yourself and your own core values.

Expansion of your personality and life structure continues as you approach 40, a period of very active psychological change and gathering of mental force. The early forties are often unstable and uncomfortable for you both personally and in the marriage relationship. Time, once disregarded, now demands that you come to terms with it in the sense that what is done is done. The die is cast. Family and work continue to focus your energy. Your friends and family increase in importance although an active social life may now seem less important. You may have regrets for

"mistakes in raising the children" but it is difficult to separate what influence you had from the impact of the times.
Your children once cherished as extensions of yourself now
have become young adults and are seen as individuals in
their own right.

Money, so bothersome in your thirties, may have become less important. If you are educating college age children, money pressure may continue for awhile. Otherwise life
settles down. There is a feeling that it is too late to make
major changes — a reconciliation ensues *of what is with what
might have been.* By 50 and in the years that follow, there is
a mellowing of relationships and feelings. You are satisfied
with your children for the most part and you no longer
blame your own parents as the cause of your own personality
problems. Increasingly you are focusing on what you have
accomplished in half a century and you no longer push
yourself to achieve in the same way. "Human" experiences
become more important, sharing the joys, sorrows and confusions and everyday life, the precious moments of contact
and deep feeling.

During the sixties, one or both of you face the crisis of
retirement from work that for so long has structured much
of your time. This is truly one of the most stressful periods in
the marriage as each of you adjust to a different time frame
of being together and finding meaningful interests to focus
your quite considerable energy. Many community volunteer
programs are discovering the "Gray Power" — resources and
rich life experience of people in this age group.

With the seventies death becomes more of a presence
and there is a sense of time running out. You are more
aware of the pattern of occurrences in every human life —
birth, death, illness, love and war and impelled to make
sense of them and peace within the facts of your own life.
There is an urgency to find meaning in perspective. Often
the bond with your partner is so deep during this phase that
neither too long survives the loss of the other.

Finding Your life's Meaning Through Marriage

The ordinary experiences of your everyday life, the coming and growth of children, job problems and moves, illnesses and death of friends and relatives furnish you and your partner with situations where you can become aware of your need for each other's continuous support and nourishment. You also feel your growing capacity to provide this for one another and for your children.

In spite of the inevitable anguish that comes when two individuals struggle to make a life together, there is an exultation in loving and being loved that goes wordlessly beyond any other type of life experience. One of the most valuable aspects of marriage is that your partner can truly become your best friend—if you define friend as one who loves you in spite of knowing your faults and weaknesses and has even better dreams for your fulfillment than you have for yourself.

This knowing of each other in the worst, as well as the best of times, provides a density to each partner in the other's eyes. There is a depth of understanding of what it means to be "human." Through marriage you learn to share with a partner the major turning points of the life cycle. The range of feelings—joy, grief, loneliness, anger, hurt, trust, vulnerability, celebration—are discovered and experienced. Religious and family values are expressed and achieved with each other, with your children and in the community.

The Relation Between Marriage and the Satisfaction of Personal Needs

In the foregoing analysis of "growing up" as an adult, it is clear that times of stress and strain are inevitable to growth. Marriage is unique in its power to facilitate emotional growth primarily because marriage can satisfy the three kinds of needs we have in relation to other people—the need to belong, the need to exert control or power, and the need for affection. The importance given to any one of these needs differs from marriage to marriage and sometimes between partners.

The need to belong, to feel included means you want to attract attention and interest, to feel yourself distinct, specific and individual. You want to be acknowledged and recognized even when there is not a strong emotional expression. You hunger to be fully seen and accepted as you are.

The need to exert control involves decision making between you and your partner, the use of power, influence on one another and authority of knowledge rather than position. This actually involves a continuum of possible satisfactions from a desire to control the other, and therefore your future, to a feeling of need to be controlled, to have responsibility lifted from yourself. You also express control in the ways you behave when your partner is trying to influence you. Being independent and rebellious indicates a lack of willingness to be controlled while you show various degrees of accepting control by complying, submitting, asking for direction. Control doesn't have to be obvious. You experiment and learn the ways of sharing control with your partner. And while you do, it often seems uncomfortable, even stormy. But each of you grows clearer about your power. There is a relation between this need to use power and marital role agreements in order to get things done, to achieve your goals.

Marriage promises the potential for affection more than any other relationship since you can feel most valued and individual, most intensely alive, when you have the sense of closeness associated with belonging, of loving and being loved.

However, you may have an ideal of companionship and sharing in marriage that does not meet most people's reality and might be realized in other ways. Ideals deflect energy when they screen out possibilities in the actual relationships you do have. Affection is always a one-to-one matter, for it is personal and emotional. It can develop in any existing relationship with increasing openness to the other person. A deepening relationship through the years with one other person transforms the experience of loving. The difference is expressed in the two statements: "I love you because I need you," which becomes "I need you because I love you."

The second statement comes from a state of consciousness called into existence by love and in contrast to ordinary consciousness always has a creative element. It creates in your loved partner a self-knowing of being loved, therefore lovable, love-worthy and self-accepting. This permits him/her to develop as a distinct and individual personality. You each came to marriage with a huge untapped potential of abilities, talents, capacities and resources which lies dormant unless called out, developed by your union.

The experience of loving is an experience of your *own* awakening, your own deepening awareness of meaning. Loving opens you to more aspects of yourself and of loving. Dynamic, continually creative ongoing encounter with your partner—with all the hangups and the differences—forces you to know yourself, your limitations. The experience of loving also brings out new parts of each of you and a greater sense of wholeness. Because you are a loving person you need the other to receive your love. You are not solely concerned with gratifying your needs and satisfying your drives. In your deepest human reality, you reach out beyond yourself toward a meaning you want to fulfill and toward another human being you want to lovingly encounter.

Examining the ways in which these needs for inclusion, power and affection are expressed and met in your marriage can be a useful device for strengthening it. Identifying deficiencies does not necessarily mean an unhealthy marriage. The emphasis, or lack of it, in any one area has much to do with the values of the two of you as individuals.

Suggested Exercises

Needs for Belonging, Power and Affection. Begin by arranging to have some quiet time to reflect and think about your needs and the strengths and resources which are a part of your marriage. Think back. What are the highlights of your marriage? What drew you to your partner in the first place? What draws you now? How do you acknowledge this? How aware is your partner of what you value in him/her? How do you know?

When do you feel most distinct, specifically individual? How does your partner recognize and relate to this aspect of you? What is your decision making process? Who exerts control in which areas? When? How? How much responsibility do you personally like to carry? What are your priorities and when they differ from your partner's what happens? How do you express your affection? How do you ask for it? How does your partner express, ask for affection? Is it usually in the context of sex with your partner? How do you express affection with other persons?

Marriage Strengths. Now take paper and list the positives, the resources, the assets in your marriage. List as many as you can. Remember that what seems a problem may hide a strength, e.g., arguing for hours sometimes means you are able to talk over problems and share your feelings fully and freely. It may also indicate you care enough about each other to keep working at a problem until both of you are satisfied.

Don't try to complete your list at one time. Think about it for a day or so and add your further thoughts with examples and specific events and happenings. Ask your partner to do the same and compare. Take as long a time as you need to discuss them. Look over the following outline and notice whether any of these are actually in your marriage but you may not have thought of them as strengths:

1. Observing birthdays, anniversaries, personal traditions and rituals.

2. Attending community functions, participating together in local and community organizations.

3. Sharing your interests, reading matter and curiosity with one another and encouraging the other's creative expression.

4. Enjoying fun and recreational experiences together.

5. Sensitivity to one another's needs for warmth, affection, love.

6. Enjoying lovemaking together.

7. Having and enjoying friends and relatives together and separately.

8. Being honest and talking things out with one another.

9. Being able to talk over and share spiritual experiences.

10. Giving encouragement and support to one another in daily work and special difficulties.

11. Being able to organize and do things together, flexibly taking over the other's responsibilities when indicated.

When you finish, discuss with your partner what you have learned and what the experience meant to you, what strengths you want to develop further.

His Strengths—Her Strengths. **Dr.** Herbert Otto's research on human potentialities indicates that fewer than one out of 110 persons ever take time to list their personality strengths and on being asked, most people will list three times as many weaknesses as strengths. This reflects a decidedly lopsided understanding of self and even less consciousness of our dormant capacities and talents—our potential.

Most of us have hidden talents or abilities which can be found and developed if we wish. Often it takes only the recognition and encouragement of a person who cares to start your process of unfolding. Awareness of your own and your partner's potentialities will give you a more positive self-concept and add a vital healthy spark to your marriage. Begin this experience by writing for five minutes what you see as your personality resources or strengths. Think about what others see and value in you, as strong points. What do you do well? Be honest. Recognize and acknowledge abilities which you know you have. You may have to cope with your cultural conditioning against conceit by contending with an inner voice that insists "but that isn't so much." With practice you can acquire the easy, open acceptance of your strengths which is a characteristic of the creative self-actualizing person.

Review the hobbies and crafts you have been interested in, any type of dancing, writing, painting, sculpture, ability to improvise music, etc. Good health represents a strength. How do you maintain it? List your self-education apart from the formal type in school, your organized reading, your years of experience in particular forms of work, your ability to relate to coworkers, pride in accomplishment, your special aptitudes, having hunches which usually turn out right, follow through, having a green thumb, mechanical ability, sales ability, ability to develop close personal relationships, intellectual curiosity, openness to new ideas, recognizing and enjoying beauty and using this ability to enhance your home or physical environment, organizational ability and experience, ability to live the religious values you believe in, ability to receive as well as give affection, being able to feel a wide range of emotions and empathy for others, humor, being able to laugh at yourself, to take risks, to get things done, to always look well-groomed. Note it all.

Now take another sheet and note what you see as your partner's strengths. Share these sheets with your partner when and if he/she so desires. For best results, do it when both of you are in a good mood and not pressed for time. When possible in discussing your partner's strengths give instances. "You're very patient and even tempered. You remember that incident with Mother and Aunt Milly last year. You were so patient and caring and never lost your temper. I really admired that but never got around to telling you."

Avoid any discussion of shortcomings or problems. Don't discount what you are hearing even if there are moments when you feel slightly uncomfortable. By sharing together how you felt when you were the focus during the experience once it is over, you have an opportunity for increased self-awareness and clarification of feelings. In the days that follow, a good follow-through is to verbally acknowledge, appreciate the strengths that you are aware of in your partner.

These exercises are designed to broaden your awareness of your own personality strengths, the positive aspects of your marriage and the resources and the potential of your partner. With greater awareness, development is encouraged and your marriage grows.

Chapter VII

Crisis and Reconnecting: Therapy of a Marriage

How can YOU know who is the best person for you when you want help? You want a person who is professionally competent and is suited to dealing with your particular personalities and problems. Basic training requirements are necessary for licensing and you can call the professional on the telephone to ask about his/her training, experience, theoretical orientation and method before setting up an appointment.

To attempt to define marriage therapy takes either courage or foolhardiness or perhaps a bit of both. It is a phenomenon of our time, complex, dynamic and in evolution. Marriage therapy is complex in terms of the varied knowledges which feed it, the ethical commitments that infuse it, the special conditions of its practice, its objectives and ends and the skills used. It is a living event and as such almost cannot be contained within a definition. The nucleus of the event is this: a couple with a problem in their relationship come to a place where a professional helps them by a given process.

Who is this couple?

Any couple who share a household and a commitment to one another. One or both partners finds himself or herself in need of help in some aspect of social/emotional living with his or her partner.

What is the problem?

The problem arises from some unmet need or accumulation of frustrations or maladjustments and sometimes all of these together. It threatens the couple's living situation or the effectiveness of their efforts to deal with it. In times of stress, hostility and buried resentments emerge even in basically satisfactory marriages. Help may be needed to reestablish collaboration.

What is the place?

The place is sometimes a family agency, sometimes the social service department of an institution such as a hospital. Sometimes it is the office of a licensed marriage, child and family counselor, sometimes the office of a psychologist, a psychiatrist, a minister or even a lawyer who specializes in family law. These professionals have varied skills in dealing with human beings experiencing problems in the management of their personal lives.

What is the process?

The process is essentially one of problem solving. This does not imply that the counselor focuses on the problems alone. It is rather that life itself is a problem solving process of continuous change and movement in which human beings work to achieve maximum satisfaction. The couple need help when, for some reason, their normal efforts are ineffective or blocked. Underneath the overt complaint — lack of communication, sexual incompatibility, competitive discounting of one another, or whatever — the block may be hidden. It may be in a lack of material resources, such as the young couple living with in-laws, where lack of privacy and financial stresses trigger emotional problems. This underlying reality must be understood as the context influencing how their problems can be worked with.

A couple may lack knowledge of the facts of a problem or of ways of meeting it, such as the meaning of a wife's postpartum depression following the birth of a baby. The counselor may supply necessary knowledge and facilitate the use of specific resources such as a visiting nurse program.

The problem between them may seem overwhelming when a couple is depleted, drained of emotional or physical energy. Yet they know they have to pull together to plan and to act according to plan. When there is illness, overwork or emotional exhaustion, the ability to "see straight," think clearly and organize something may be at low ebb. In these situations, the counselor may work to provide physical or psychological supports to restore equilibrium in the home before the couple can begin to face up and tackle their problems. Social workers, in particular, are familiar with a range of services such as temporary homemakers and other community resources for use when the couples are under severe stress.

In addition to problems within the relationship such as infidelity or threat of separation, added family problems can arouse high feelings—so strong that reason is overwhelmed—grief at a death, delinquency in a child, or anxiety over a serious illness. Sometimes these overwhelming feelings are "over-reactions" caused by the problem bringing to life old dormant feelings from losses in the past. In such times, thought processes, delicately tuned as they are to emotions, become clouded. The counselor works to get the feelings expressed and to lessen the impact of these varied problems so the couple can begin to "see straight," to analyze the situation between them (what each is contributing) and to think of alternatives.

Finally the problem may lie primarily within one partner. That is, he/she may have become subject to emotions that chronically over a long period have governed thinking and action. In the language of subpersonalities, it is as if one personality had totally taken over and all other aspects of the person were repressed. Somewhere in this person's past a problem of great emotional import to him/her was left unsolved, pushed under but far from finished. It affects the way he sees, thinks about and tries to deal with his partner and his present day life, especially if some part of this resembles his original problem. In this situation, individual work as well as work with the relationship is needed.

The marriage counselor engages and works with both partners' individual motives, feelings, attitudes, ideas and behavior as they relate to the problems they are experiencing as a couple. The professional has some systematic idea of how to get hold of the problem, how to understand it and then how to work on it. This is based in his/her theoretical orientation and experience.

A Gestalt therapist, for example, will pay close attention to evidence of conflicting wishes or impulses *within* each partner and the projections made to the other partner. The Transactional analyst tends to look for evidence of parent, adult and child ego states as they are manifested in behavior and verbal transactions. He/she watches for the "games" or patterns of interaction of these ego states between the partners which prevent intimacy. Conjoint family therapy focuses on the family as a system of interaction and pays close attention to communication styles as well as discrepant content of the messages they send to one another. The orthodox psychoanalytic approach places emphasis on unresolved unconscious conflicts. The Jungians tend to look at the conflicts originating in personality type differences, in perception and judgment and also at the "fit" of masculine and feminine elements within each partner, and their level of development.

Names of marriage therapists can be obtained from professional associations such as the Society for Clinical Social Work, the Family Service Association, from your physician, your minister, even the Yellow Pages of the telephone book. Assuming you can locate one or more licensed professionals who have the orientation you prefer, you still have to *choose* that therapist. All forms of psychotherapy, including marital therapy, are more art than science and the personality, the stability, the skill of the therapist are all important. There is one other variable more difficult to describe — your inner sense that this is a person *you* and your partner can work with. If you do not feel this trust, contact someone else.

Therapy can help sick marriages. It costs time and money. Initially when you start, you experience a "honeymoon" period of goodwill but things will get worse before they get better. It is inevitable that when feelings which have been suppressed are expressed, the other partner has reactions of hurt and defensive anger. As greater clarity is gained about the function of the conflict and the needs of each partner, these reactions diminish and a consciously agreed on working contractual relationship can be established.

The Marriage Contract

The concept of a "marriage contract" between you and your spouse is extremely useful to understand your interactions. It exists but probably was not a conscious agreement. You want to understand your interactions in terms of how they "fit" or conflict with what you each expect and what you each feel obliged to provide for your partner. The term "contract" refers to your expressed and *unexpressed* ideas of your obligations within the marital relationship. It refers also to the benefits you expect to get from marriage in general and from your partner in particular. What must be emphasized is the *reciprocal* aspect of the contract. What you expect to give is related to what you expect to receive in exchange. Your contract can cover every conceivable aspect of family life — relationships with friends, achievements, power, sex, leisure time, money, children, and so on. The degree to which your marriage satisfies your own and your partner's contractual expectations is an important determinant of the quality of your marriage.

The "terms" of the contract are determined by deep needs and wishes within each of you. It goes almost without saying that some of these are healthy and realistic and others are unreal and contradictory wishes. What is important in this context is that each of you may be aware of his/her own needs and wishes to varying degrees. But you do not usually think that your attempts to fill your partner's needs implicitly assumes that your partner will then be obliged to fulfill your needs. Furthermore, you may be quite unaware of your partner's implicit expectations. Each of you may be assuming mutual agreement regarding his/her own contract when in fact there is not. Nevertheless, you behave as if an actual contract existed and you and your partner are obliged to fulfill its terms. When significant aspects of the contract cannot be fulfilled, as is inevitable when one partner may be unaware of them, the disappointed partner may react with rage, hurt or depression. It is as though a real agreement had been broken. This is particularly true if one partner feels he/she has fulfilled his obligations but that his/her partner has not.

The sources of contractual difficulties vary. Sometimes it is that you each have different ideas about the role of a wife, the role of a husband. One of you may have an inner conflict with your own needs and wishes and the contract will reflect these conflicts and contradictions. For example, you may want closeness but when it happens, you feel engulfed and want distance. One of you may frustrate the expectations of the other in a specific area because this aspect of marriage arouses a great deal of anxiety in you. Unfortunately, a sadistic partner may enjoy a sense of power from frustrating the other. There are other contracts which fail because they are based on unrealistic expectations—the partner simply does not have the capacity to gratify them. The lack may be in the partner or in a fantasy that no relationship can fulfill in reality.

It is useful to consider the content of the marriage contract on three levels:

I. *Conscious, verbalized:* This would include what each of you told your partner about his/her expectations in clearly understandable language. These probably formed your choice to marry the other. The reciprocal aspects of these expectations may not have been recognized.

II. *Conscious, but not verbalized:* Each of you had expectations, plans, beliefs, fantasies which differed from level I only in that they were not verbalized, usually because of some sense of fear or shame connected with their disclosure.

III. *Beyond awareness:* This includes all those desires and needs, often contradictory and unrealistic, of which you have no awareness, i.e. the hidden agendas of the subpersonalities. These may contain some degree of conflict with what you hold at level I or II.

The following chart outlines the progress of a relationship from the initial sharing of information and expectations to the making of a marriage commitment and stable family life until one individual begins to feel some pinch. The chart indicates that there will be times when one of you feels his/her needs are not being cared for in the marriage as set up. There has to be some way of sharing this perception and renegotiating for more time or space or whatever. Otherwise, crisis occurs.

Anxiety increases with crisis and this is often the best time to use professional help with your marriage. When the crisis is serious, there seem to be three options: divorce, return to the way things were (which does away with the confusion and anxiety but doesn't deal with the issues) OR to renegotiate, which involves going back to redefining why

INFORMATION AND EXPECTATIONS/COMMITMENT
CRISIS AND RENEGOTIATION IN MARRIAGE

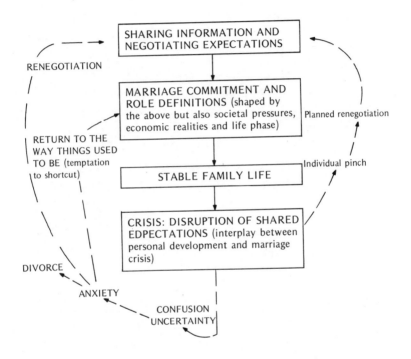

you want to live together and what you now understand your
needs to be.

Marriage therapy will focus on the relationship and
most sessions will be jointly with your partner, either as a
couple alone with the counselor or in a couples group usually co-led by a man-woman therapist team. One of the
primary functions of the marriage counselor will be to
observe the behavior between you and your partner, to help
you become aware of the "rules" you've developed, almost

unnoticed, to govern your interactions. These are based in the implicit contracts mentioned earlier. For instance, you may each be aware that the other has critical thoughts, but neither really airs them "to avoid hassling." Or the father is ostensibly in charge of disciplining the children, but in fact the mother is the one who decides who is punished for what and the father is simply the executioner, a role which means problems for everyone. The therapist may suggest an alternative rule to try. The effects are observed. Sometimes the counselor may help you to see your conflicting values in a different light. Rather than arguing about who is right about over or under disciplining the children, you may recognize the team aspect of your parenting—that one of you is helping the other not to be too permissive while the other helps not to be too restrictive.

One of the most important functions a marriage counselor can fulfill is helping you to assess the strengths and assets in your marriage. A neutral third party can help you put labels on the reasons you stay together, something you tend to overlook in times of stress. The marriage counselor encourages you to risk making more of the level II contract explicit with one another and to negotiate realistic ways for both of you to have your needs met or to achieve mutually agreed on compromises.

Sometimes one or both partners need a few individual sessions to work through inner problems which affect the marriage. A description of one marriage follows.

There is no such thing as a typical marriage. The situation of Frank and Sally is used to illustrate some of the issues and the interplay of the different needs and understandings between two partners who are basically well suited to one another, care deeply about their family, but who have gotten into some mutually destructive patterns. The crisis and the resolution involved six months treatment in a couple group and ten days of intensive individual work with Sally. A follow-up session two months after the conclusion of treatment confirmed the changes which had occurred, but suggested that a short period of additional work with Frank would be useful.

Onset of Crisis

Frank and Sally have been married for fifteen years. Frank, a prosperous businessman, thinks of himself as the type of man other people instinctively turn to for good advice. He is pleased with the "family" feeling among his office staff. Sally recently returned to college as she feels her three sons are sufficiently grown not to need her so constantly at home. The marriage which followed a passionate courtship in their early twenties, has tempered over the years to a placid relationship quite comfortable to Sally, although not so to Frank. He has expressed his dissatisfaction repeatedly. He feels that he just does not matter sufficiently to Sally. When they are together, he experiences a deep feeling of resentment toward her. He is ill at ease, frustrated and in a smoldering sort of way, angry at her. He thinks about this often with a sense of shame and guilt, for he cannot understand why his frustration and annoyance should be so strong. He recognizes that she is a fine mother and a sweet and thoughtful person. "I really have little excuse for being so angry at her so much of the time, especially since the things which annoy me are so trivial."

For instance, Sally has had a cleaning woman for the past ten years. The hall rug looks dirty to Frank, as dirty when the cleaning woman has been there as when he left it in the morning. He specifically asked Sally to see that it was taken care of. "Sally, for God's sake, I've asked you to have Elsie clean this entrance for three months. Why can't you see that she does it?"

Sally looks at him somewhat maternally, shakes her head and smiles patiently. "But darling, you know how nervous she is. I just can't hurt her feelings. I tell her . . . that's how it is." Frank replies, "I know you are busy with school, the children and your volunteer work but I want a clean house. Get someone else to help her if you won't fire her."

Sally's eyes grow watery. She bites her lips and says, "Frank, I'll do the best I can but that's no solution. Anything I can do to help you by being a good wife is what I want to do." She makes the bed hastily before leaving for her first class. Frank drives to the office, his stomach growling. A throbbing tension is beginning to build up at the back of his neck and spreading up into the occipital region. He feels rather bitter toward the world at large — but knows vaguely that it is related to his wife.

What has characterized their conversation is the lack of a completed transaction. No decision has been made. Sally's position is that she will do anything Frank desires, but his past experience with her is that *she will not*. He is completely frustrated and does not know how to deal with the situation. As it is with the vacuuming incident, so it has been with gardening, with planning vacations, dinner arrangements, etc.

Comment: There is a place in the best of marriages for occasional bluntness, rudeness, even an out and out fight. At times we all let our relationships become complacent and limited by incomplete transactions. In taking a position with an occasional explosion, the limits of the relationship are clarified. Just as there is no making an omelet without breaking eggs, you cannot make a marriage without breaking some of your partner's expectations and complacencies. In Sally's view, she is mollifying an unreasonable man and delaying his demands by placating him. She is unaware that by behaving inconsiderately while *appearing* to be considerate, thoughtful and patient, she is slowly driving Frank to distraction. He never knows definitely what he can realistically expect from her. She appears to be willing but her actions convey another message: "I don't think it is necessary" or something of that sort. Frank is as culpable as Sally because her benevolent tone sidetracks him. Possibly the circumstances of his own rearing have made him susceptible to apparent benevolence and his experience with Sally has reinforced this response. Possibly he avoids a showdown because he senses that some reciprocal demand would be made on him that he prefers not to hear.

What is needed to change this pattern is that each make a special effort to listen to the other's statements, and when a statement is not absolutely clear, the confused partner must draw it out. He/she should indicate, for example, that the meaning or the context is unclear or that the tone of voice seems to imply something that does not fit with the words. Frank must reply with something like: "Perhaps I'm misunderstanding you. What I hear you saying is that you refuse to insist that Elsie do the work for which she is paid, and would rather that I put up with this dirty entrance way than hire someone else to complete the work. Is that what you mean?" Then he must "hang in there" in the face of any further rationalizations until a clear agreement is reached how and when the hall will be cleaned. This did not happen in the precrisis period.

Crisis

One night, Sally unexpectedly overheard Frank on the telephone and realized from his tone, which changed from one of intimacy to brusk business when he realized that she had come in, that he must be involved with another woman. Sally was stunned. Frank initially denied it, then admitted that this was so. A "fatherly" relationship with one of his office "family" had recently deepened to a more intimate affair. For the next few weeks their life was in an upheaval. They considered divorce. The implications — tearing apart the life they had built together and the effect on their children made this unacceptable.

The "cold war" of mutual isolation between them was unendurable and they talked of "open marriage" as an alternative. Sally turned to a close business friend client of Frank who was divorced and attentive to her. Frank overtly approved of this. The détente continued for six months until Frank admitted that this was not what he wanted at all. His relationship with Sally was the one which really mattered. Sally agreed, but said she felt they could not go back without understanding why this happened and unless they decided they truly wanted to stay together. She realized that part of her reluctance to get a divorce was a fear of being alone rather than a wish to be with Frank, so she suggested marriage therapy.

Couple Group Therapy

When a couple is struggling to create a mutually satisfying relationship between them, the atmosphere is nutritious. Within a small group of 4–5 couples, a potent milieu for change is created. Healthy struggling in each couple relationship is the main target for the group's therapeutic work. Reciprocity in relatedness more than such things as kindness, caring and generosity, carries the greatest influence on human behavior. Each person wants to be seen uniquely as he/she is, even if all of his qualities are not valued by the other(s). Each person potentially controls the happenings in his/her own life, but at least one other person is required for their release. There is no substitute for that needed other person with whom one struggles for union and separateness. The other couples in the group are used as qualified sounding boards and as witnesses to the personal attempt to grasp what must be changed. Each person in such a group learns to look at the problems of others in an OBJECTIVE manner. And learns to listen. And think.

The issue is fundamental change, not minor adjustments like learning not to be sarcastic. Walter Kempler puts it succinctly in his *Principles of Gestalt Family Therapy:* "Change is forged in the fires of struggle. Casual conversation provides knowledge and understanding and, at best, can bring one into a conflict zone. But before there can be change, there must be struggle and before there can be struggle, there must be discord." The process begins and continues through *relating* — recounting oneself, telling and engaging in one's struggle with the other. Hearing one's own awareness as it passes through the listening others and returns to his/her own ear, is the essential ingredient.

Sally and Frank were active participants in the couple group process for the three month contract which started with a session extended over a weekend, and continued with a weekly two hour session. They continued with another group for an additional three months when the first one was finished. Frank's perceptions of other couples' feelings and problems were sensitive and accurate. About their own, however, he and Sally both seemed curiously blocked. For example, in the first session describing what was wrong between them:

Frank: We don't know what's wrong. We just don't have any feeling for each other any longer. We have thought of divorce, but we really don't want to.

Therapist (to Sally): Where does your version differ?

Sally: It doesn't.

Male Group Member (to Frank): Tell her your fantasy of the girl who could "turn you on." What would she do and how would she behave that would be different from Sally's behavior?

In response to this digging, Frank's expectations of what his wife's contract should include emerged. He felt he should be the most important person in Sally's life. Her care and primary concern for him should be always apparent. She should enjoy doing things with him regardless of who else was there. She is very sexually attractive to him, but she should want to heighten the chemistry between them by making him feel that he, too, has an impact on her. Almost as an afterthought he added that she should be a competent mother, which he acknowledged Sally to be, and she should manage the house in such a way that he would find nothing to complain about.

Longings, desires, wants, needs, wishes, hopes—these are the field from which conflict and fulfillment rise. The therapist searches for the conflicting desire in Sally:

Therapist (to Sally): Tell him why you no longer want to be sexual with him.

Sally: I don't know. It is just unpleasant to me now.

Therapist (pressing): Tell him what is unpleasant about his behavior.

Sally: When you say things like that, I feel angry and turned off completely. I feel like my every word and action is being watched like a hawk. I feel smothered—like I have no separate space for *me*. You are exactly like my father. You want me to behave only as you want. Neither of us is "turned on" sexually and know it so we each dare not approach the other. The tension builds up in me to talk after nothing is said for so long. I instigate the talk. There is defensiveness and anger on both our parts, especially me, and we are miserable. The next morning you are always apologetic and loving (much holding on, head stroking, etc.) and we agree we have to be more understanding with each other— but nothing changes.

Separateness in a couple relationship does not imply the willingness to stand alone but the ability to stand apart from one another, when necessary, while struggling for a union which better serves both partners. Sally is struggling for differentiation. Only when she and Frank have a better notion of their separate realities can they achieve a more integrated union.

As the group session goes on, a picture of the marriage embodying a type of parent-child relationship grows. Frank refuses to answer any of Sally's questions about their financial situation although she suspects he is worried. He reacts to her questions as if she were attacking him.

It becomes clear that each is acting out patterns shaped by the past. Frank had received (and bought) strong injunctions from his mother that no matter what he did in life, it would not be enough to please her. From his father he had learned to be frightened of and to control his anger, usually venting it only in the guise of long intellectualized "explorations of an issue," overwhelming the other person with words, but always feeling very empty and depressed himself afterwards. Sally recognized that she had received a strong "Don't be you. Be my picture of you" message from her father. This was what she was hearing now from Frank and she fought it. As she fought, he in turn, heard his mother's message that he could not please her. As a result he felt depressed and developed a "smothered" anger of which he was only partly aware.

As these connections were discovered, it became possible to differentiate the past influences and feelings from the present relationship.

Sally: My father was a very irrational man about money. He deprived himself and mother at really important times and spent it unwisely at others—a very expensive vacuum cleaner which mother didn't like, volumes of books from a door to door salesman, a deep freezer, etc. Mother nearly always felt she had to explain, rationalize or hide money she spent, especially on herself.

I realize that one of the things that I fell in love with in Frank was his very *generous* attitude about money, his comme ci, comme ca belief: "Sure we can handle that, it will be O.K." This seemed such a *relief* to me. He filled very nicely the kind father role I needed and I adored him for that . . . I suspect my feelings of loss, confusion and disappointment deepen Frank's feeling of inadequacy which must have been there all along, and was the reason he jumped at the chance to prove his love and worth to us by providing money and all the material things we thought we wanted.

They each explored their feeling responses to the financial issues. Frank thought he should be able to provide for the family's financial wants without involving them in his business problems. These were complex and he did not want the feeling of having to "explain" or justify himself to Sally. It was painful, made him feel "put down," depressed, inadequate.

His financial affairs he felt to be his, not the family's. Sally had colluded with this attitude in her wish to be taken care of but now she had grown to the point of wanting a collaborative marriage. Each recognized how he/she set the other up as an oppressor:

> You frustrate me.
> You overwhelm me.
> You are *too* understanding.
> The victim is always me.
> The victim is always innocent.

They now had enough understanding that they could identify their conflicting desires, wishes, hopes for what they were and struggle with one another rather than experience the continuous dull, gray pain of boredom and indifference, loneliness and depression, frustration and rage, bitterness and chronic discontent. They no longer needed the group to witness and develop their skills. Sally, however, recognized that in too many situations Frank seemed to wear her father's face and she felt a need to disentangle the anger she felt toward her father so it would no longer contaminate her marital relationship. She and I then arranged for a ten-day period of intensive individual treatment.*

*This form of therapy is more fully described in my book *The Inward Journey*.

During this period she lived apart from the family and following a morning session with me, spent most of her time with art processes or writing. It was a time of clearing away old self images, of finishing unfinished business with both her parents, of identifying recurring patterns in her behavior and looking at the underlying questions she had been attempting to answer. And finally, she looked at herself, her changing body image, varying energy levels, talents, interests that had been laid aside and educational possibilities for the person she now felt herself to be.

The first day she examined the subpersonalities she knew about:

Sally-Ann: sweet, endearing, model child, too perfect (a hypocrite with a Southern drawl) hiding the weeping, frightened, doubting little girl who needs verbal reassurance and cuddling.

Sal (Girl): fun loving daughter, playmate, sister, wholesome, all-American girl type friend.

Su-Su: endearing nickname, more sophisticated and grown-up — only known to very close friends.

Sal (Woman): sophisticated, adult and grown-up, a symbol of change in me wants to throw away the little girl who has too long been center stage.

Sarah: formal, prissy, putting on airs — when I was a child, but now I think this part may be evolving into a person I want to be.

She added the parts she would like to discover in herself:

The Researcher: I'd like to know more about the learning process and how it is affected.

The Performer: I'd like to be freer and less inhibited physically. I'd like to dance and sing and act.

The Adventurer: I'd like to experience other places and

people freely, not in my structured time-limit plan—
moving on when the purpose is right, perhaps even
earning money as I go, having much less concern about
where to stay, what to see and do and when to get back.
The Lover: I feel this part has never really developed—the
sexy, gutsy, earthy part of me.

And then she went back to the strong feelings she had about
herself in childhood, mostly embarrassment over her romantic fantasies, disturbance with her father's emotional-
ism—his anger and weeping, embarrassment with her
bedwetting which had continued to age 9, mental cringing
with her father's touch; "the worse was when he would crawl
into bed with me," and a fearfulness with her parents'
quarreling; "father being unreasonable and mother quietly
taking it."

Her father dominated the picture of her early life. She
was the oldest child and a year later a brother was born. The
parents divided their responsibilities, her father caring for
her physical needs, bathing her, playing with her, bringing
her with him on some of his work rounds. Her mother similarly cared for Sally's brother. The effect though was to
polarize the family and patterns developed in which her
father seemed to confuse who she was. He was subject to
depression and she could always cheer him up. The program was she was always to be bright and cheerful around
him. She alone knew how to manage him and he treated her
with great affection, in return for doing this. She thought
she loved him dearly, but as she grew older, she became
increasingly uncomfortable around him. He seemed to
totally disregard her mother. She had learned her lesson
well never to upset him, so she never voiced feelings which
conflicted with his.

I suggested that she bring him into the room, now, and
tell him those feelings. Sally in recounting her childhood
had been breathing very shallowly. I asked her if she noticed
that she seemed to be holding her breath when she talked to

her father. She said that ever since she had started this session on her father, she had felt her nose was stuffy. I had her do a bioenergetic exercise to deepen her breathing. I continued to remind her to breathe as she haltingly continued. I suggested she tell her father her resentments. After a long silence she began to slowly word her perceptions that her father had placed her in the position her mother should have held. He was overly affectionate to her and in incidents like his cuddling her as a teenager, she had learned to stifle her feelings, both her anger and her sexuality. Finally, with a cry of pure pain, she was flooded with tears and incoherent anger. I was her witness, my function to help her stay with and deeply experience the feelings so long repressed.

Anger at parents is a phase in therapy. It is necessary to experience it deeply in order to let it go. We all have been wounded, most often inadvertently by our parents in their fallibility, limitations, confusions, their own hurts and anxieties. Before we can see them objectively (to the extent that we ever do) and forgive them as fellow struggling humans, we have to know those hurt places that we have learned so well to hide from our own awareness, and the passionate anger that comes with our assertion of our rights. While Sally was experiencing the anger deeply, it was still necessary for her to express it, to word it as fully as she could. When our session ended this day, I suggested she write her father (now many years dead) a letter that would express *all* her feelings.

Dear Daddy:

You are a god-damn son-of-a-bitch for doing the really evil things you did to me. For your own pleasure, your own personal need, your own racket you *used* me. In my child-like innocent acceptance of being used, you took away from me what was rightfully mine — my sexuality as a woman. I was left with the ability to bestow pleassure (although even that was doubted for a long time) but you took away my ability to feel pleasure. As surely as if you had cut part of my body away—I was not a whole person.

You were selfish and demanding of me and blind to what you were doing *to* me, so engulfing was your own need.

And so, my bombastic, snivelling, sulky, sick father. I am writing you this letter to let you know that I will not be *used* by you anymore! It is time for you to *GET OFF MY BACK!*

I have now learned how to be in control— for the first time I HAVE A CHOICE! I will not be smothered by you. I am learning how to breathe and I am going to breathe in all those parts of life which you took away from me.

I will *not* be the poor little Sally victim child any longer. I am filled with *righteous indignation*—how about that for a good Christian ethic!

Surely you can understand that!

Crap—and you know it! You preached those ethics to cure your own soul and whenever it didn't help—to hell with the ethics! Well, don't come crying to me any more.

You have shit in my backyard long enough— it's full! But I'm going to start shoveling out today!!

I hope your soul is not in the same torment your mind and body were, but I couldn't possibly do anything about that anymore.

So It's time for me to stop trying to. It's time for me to grow up and put away my childish feelings of hurt and shame and uncontrol.

I feel angry about all the years I've wasted "wiping up your snivels" instead of finding out what kind of a woman I was or even that I *was* a *woman!*

And so, my dear Father, you gave me life in the beginning but you *kept* it for your own unhealthy needs, clinging like a leach!

Well, today, I'M TAKING IT BACK!!

Love,
Sally

Some of Sally's art work can be used to capsulize the rest of her treatment. Monday 2/3 is a picture of how she saw herself as she entered therapy. "I have just come out of a long dark tunnel but I am still in a cocoon. I don't know yet who or what I am." Tuesday 2/4: "a picture of the two ways I see men — either depressed and needing my caring or full of steam and demanding that I be equally turned on." "The second painting of fists is my anger at my Dad." 2/6 "I cannot accept my feelings. I think they are not justified. This gives me a boxed in feeling of having no place to go." The second picture reflects a relaxation exercise I had suggested to deepen her breathing and reconnect her to her feelings. She was to imagine breathing into and filling a balloon in her belly when she began to feel smothered. 2/7 represented her feeling of loss in relation to her mother in childhood and on 2/7 she drew her feeling as we began to explore her sexuality and her feelings toward her husband. 2/8 was the illustration of the following dream which she had dreamed two nights before:

I am the teacher of a class of children. They have been awarded some recognition for some special reason. I don't know what, something they did well. As a reward they are putting on a play for the rest of the school. The play is being acted out sort of in fits and starts, rather loose and unorganized but enthusiastically as the children have ideas, even as the audience is watching. I am in the play too but get distracted by 2 or 3 other kids to go outside to look at some black bugs crawling around in a big hole in the ground. The thought occurs to me I should get some bug spray, but then remember that the play is going on and it must be time for us to be back in it. As we rush back, sure enough it is past the time for our entrance, but the kids have thought up some good ideas to distract and keep the audience "going."

Her interpretation follows:

Thinking about the bugs in my dream: all of a sudden I remembered that I had used the word *"earthy"* is connection with the missing sexual part of me. We had described the bugs as earthy — not a dangerous but a nagging persistent problem and one that needs to be taken care of. I carried this further in my mind and on paper and it seemed to fit:

1) All the art work I had produced the whole day before was consistently about my sexuality — that was the *first* thing I wanted to show.

2) The idea of the hole — a mysterious vagina containing nagging doubts and worries?

3) The picture produced the stream from the play going past the hole — my experience of my vagina, its purpose taking only a few moments of my attention was passed by and not included in my main stream of life."

Her further reflections were that the children represented a natural free and creative child aspect of her which had been released in the intensive therapy. They were directing her attention to her feminine sexuality.

Working with images from her dreams, relating to them and connecting them to the events in her life had enabled her to recognize this emerging push toward her own wholeness. The issues with her family were largely finished and she now needed to deal with her attitudes which held a destructive element in regard to her sexuality. Much of this was connected with her fear of "letting go" which would put her into a state of emotional dependency which she connected with her father/daughter feelings of helplessness.

On 2/11 she listed the gains she was taking from therapy:

Most Important Gains From My Inward Journey

1) An awareness of my own physical expression of my uncomfortable feelings (breathing and stuffiness).

2) Realization that I could control these feelings, I was not their slave.

3) That it is all right to have those uncomfortable feelings about people you love and still love them very much because I am made up of many parts who can feel different ways.

4) If this is true for me, then it's true for everyone else in regard to me—if I can accept this in me, I must accept it in them.

5) Realization that I see everyone I care about and love as either my father or my mother, and how this need I ask of others colors my experience of that person so much that I am not able to see him as he really is, or to have real true feelings about him.

6) The parts of me (the animus, the mothering woman, the natural child, the adaptive child, the shadow (unvoiced feelings about Dad, Mother and Frank), the sexual woman and my mask.

7) *Needing* someone to love you for the parts in you that you love also. You don't really know this by just knowing they love you, you need

to know *why and why not* so there is a choice — either, or; or both, and

8) Value of art therapy and writing (also looking at dreams) is in creating an objectiveness to feelings.

9) An understanding of the collusive marriage — we both have needs for the other to fill — especially right now:

> *Frank:* that he is adequate — that he is good enough — just as Andy our son has these needs — accept his feeling as his and then help him *do* something.
>
> *Me:* that my needs *are* acceptable to Frank and not a put-down so that I won't feel smothered.

In the follow-up two months later, she identified herself a much more assertive, happier and content. There were times of really feeling "down" feelings too but this was O.K. She had continued with breathing exercises and some body work to free the tensions which for so long she used to keep herself from feeling her feelings. Frank confirmed this, but it was clear that some aspects of the "new woman" were difficult for him. His financial problems were depressing him and it was annoying to see Sally so handily coping. There were indications that Frank, too, could use a period of intensive care (therapy).

The ongoing life of the couple after therapy broadens and deepens their understanding of the gains they have made and their skill in the use of their own powers in meeting their needs. Successful union does not mean that there is always a sense of perfect fulfillment. At best one feels that all is now possible and, at worst, that life is bearable.

Suggested Exercise:

In this chapter I've referred to use of art to understand feelings. The art methods used in therapy reach different levels of the personality than words alone. The family sculpture in clay described in Chapter III is a quick way for marriage partners to understand what each may be carrying into the relationship from past family conditioning. Clay with its sensory tactile qualities has a capacity to bring out the as yet unworded. It takes you away from analyzing and speculating on the *whys* of behavior. Clay is useful in the exploration of sticky, messy, "bad" feelings. It has one other advantage. Most people do not demand of themselves that their clay product be perfect. That's not the nature of clay.

You can use a hunk of clay to express how you feel about yourself in the relationship and how you would like to feel. Don't rush. Let yourself play with the material. Push it. Poke it. Something will emerge which feels right which you can share with your partner. So often we don't know exactly *what* it is we are feeling and this can help you to become conscious of your undercurrent feelings.

A valuable exercise for marriage partners is to jointly share the painting of a picture. Try it in silence, each painting in turn. Notice how you feel as the painting takes a different twist from the one you intended. How do you react? How does the art experience reflect your everyday process in relating to each other.

Another exercise I have developed recently is to have each partner depict or symbolize his/her view of himself/herself in their individual interests, wants and growing edges. Then each paints a picture of their relationship which incorporates elements from their own and their partner's initial picture. If you try this, you can use the two pictures which result to talk further about your two different perceptions of the relationship and the place of your individual needs.

Art methods, in giving tangible form to perceptions and goals helps to start you toward them.

Chapter VIII

The Future of Marriage

Marriage has not always taken the form of one man and one woman in a mutually chosen commitment. That a man and a woman who are attracted to one another should agree to share a life, a household, common interests and commitments is one of the most satisfactory arrangements that social culture has brought into being. But it has been a long time in evolving. Marriage has reflected the changing cultures in which it has existed. From the Babylonians to our present technological age, each period influenced the structure, goals, functions and rituals of the marriages within it. In each, the family was necessary for a stable political society even as it is today. Aristotle in his treatise on Politics identified the function of the family . . . to provide an incentive for men to work and remain productive—thus helping them to make good citizens—and to promote moral development in children. It is through the family, Aristotle argued, that children receive their fundamental education regarding religion, personal discipline and political values.

Today, the structure and function of society and its primary institutions are under stress, a reflection of pro-

133

found changes taking place in children and young people. The center of these changes, the family, is showing a more rapid and radical transformation than it has undergone in centuries. A crucial side effect is the failure of thousands of young adults to be constructively integrated into our society. Research shows that the forces of disorganization arise primarily not from within the family but from the circumstances in which the family finds itself and by the way of life that is imposed by those circumstances. The sociologists have in mind government and business decisions about urban planning and transportation which have the effect of isolation. The separation of residential and business areas, the breakdown of neighborhoods, zoning ordinances, consolidated schools, supermarkets, television, separate patterns of social life for different age groups, the working mother, delegation of children to day care centers, all these promote isolation, the separation of adults and children from meaningful activities and involvement with one another.

Isolation and alienation threaten the security of marriage whether considered on the level of the individual, the couple or the family in relation to the community. The mobility which characterizes our society has meant a loss of everyday family connections and childhood friends. Individuals now require more companionship from their marriage partners. This is particularly true for women. Fifty years ago it was not uncommon to have at least one other adult in the home besides the parents. The hunger for companionship was not focused so acutely on the marriage relationship.

Changes are taking place in the ways men and women relate to one another, ways which are more inclusive and sensitive to feeling needs and growth possibilities of each partner. Consciousness *is* rising. The conflicts clarify the issues for those who can sustain them. But the issues opened up by the women's liberation movement are painful and confusing. Women are pressing not only for companionship but also for presence in every field of human interest. They want recognition of their abilities, full human citizenship rights and economic equality. The implications pose a fundamental challenge to the traditional structure of the family, the role of the man and how the young shall be integrated into our society. Women's protests, however, are of equity and common sense against a patriarchial tradition of relatively recent origin in the history of mankind. They are *not* protests against the institution of marriage. It is the association and cooperation between the sexes which lies at the root of all social culture and the sentiments of civilized humanity.

The structure of marriage has been changing during the past hundred years from a norm of one marriage expected to last throughout a lifetime, to an increased acceptance of the possibility of divorce, and for some, serial monogamy. In recent years we have heard more of such alternatives to marriage as simply "living together" as long as the partners are interested. Or joining a commune where one can experience something less intense than the demands of a commitment to a single partner. Some marriage partners have experimented with "open marriage" arrangements where each is free to seek and experience other relationships with or without sexual involvement. The danger, in my view, lies in the tendency to invest less in such relationships, holding back from the risks and the pain of confrontation. Trust and emotional security are easily undermined. These relationships which involve a sequence of partners share a similarity with homosexuality in that there is a large investment in personal sexual attractiveness. There is a tendency to "hang on" to the problems and possibilities of a phase of the life cycle associated with the early twenties. This, rather than moving on to a more responsible relationship to the community, a commitment to one partner and one's own wholeness. Love and playing at love is still distinct from marriage.

The majority of young persons "living together" are in fact fairly committed to each other and exclusively so. They seem to be ending up in marriage when the practical realities of buying a home or raising a child begin to be felt.

Many cultures have sanctioned a series of more or less serious love affairs for the young before settling into a commitment to a lasting partnership. Parenthood is the pivotal point in the anatomy of a marriage. Bronislaw Malinowski, a great anthropologist, claims that women will have the last word in deciding what the future of marriage is to be. Women now claim freedom but they still continue to have children and desire to have children. He says the future of marriage hangs on three questions: Now that women have freedom in conception will they still be interested in maternity? Then, will a woman, however intelligent, feminist and progressive consent to undergo the dangers and hardships of childbirth and give her child to any type of communal care other than her own? The last question is whether she will choose to have the man she chooses as father of her child continue as her mate to share the responsibilities of child rearing.

I disagree with Malinowski on only one point. Marriage and family imply that there is an innate need in the male to face his responsibilities and share in the process of reproduction and continuity of culture. The danger is that disidentified young men will not make this choice. Even for men who make the choice, fatherhood is often an unclear role. If bread winning is not the essential male task, what is it that women cannot do equally well? Traditionally men have oriented their sons in the tasks of a man and have represented and interpreted the reality of the world "out there" to the family while the mother was primarily responsible for the inner feeling and nurturing of the family. What now? "Men's Lib" seems like a joke but masculine consciousness raising is a real need in our society.

The growing phenomenon of homosexuality needs to be understood independently of one's feeling about homosexuality and free of the bias created by automatic labeling. What happens that allows some people to retain their male gender identity but have a strong feminine identification and a male object choice? In our society we have tended to take masculine identity for granted. Boys are expected to pursue girls. Their masculine ego identity is thought to be totally secure. If a man can't satisfy a woman, he judges himself inadequate. Men are given no quarter in their efforts to achieve a masculine identity. Yet for a boy raised in a neighborhood where the men are largely absent in work that he does not know directly, where his school teachers are women during his formative years, forming a clear masculine identity is not easy.

Studies published in the *New England Journal of Medicine* in 1971 indicated a biological basis for homosexuality in pregnant mothers with adrenocortical deficiencies. In adult homosexuals, hormone levels are quite low and sperm counts vary according to the degree of homosexuality as measured on the Kinsey scale. If the studies stand the test of further investigation, homosexuality will be viewed as a condition of physical malfunction which leads to maladaptive behavior from a biological and evolutionary point of view. Other studies indicate that homosexuality has a further basis in patterns of child-rearing (Paul J. Fink, M.D., "Homosexuality: Illness or Lifestyle," *Journal of Sex and Marital Therapy*, Spring 1975). The mother's time commitments are such that she has few other avenues for channeling her feelings of caring and love and she finds this boy-child unusually attractive. The child imitates her behaviors and the father, if present, does not object. The boy with lowered androgen levels because of the intrauterine endocrine factor has lower aggressivity and his earliest learned social skills are those more typical of girls. The father, if present, experiences rejection from his son and deems him a "mama's boy." The emotional distance between them continues to increase because of the boy's low interest in his father's activities. The boy's identification with feminine skills poses an obstacle to same-sex peer integration during the first few years of school and causes him to be labeled a sissy. Fathers are either passive or absent in an empty angry marriage which is preserved. Homosexuality is not a condition of shame or degradation but neither is it a liberated life style alternative to marriage.

Whatever will develop in the long run, marriages continue to be made and the majority of these marriages do endure. But there is presently a trend toward having no children, or one or two at the maximum. This means more children raised as only children, with whatever personality implications this may have. Also they will have fewer role models in terms of uncles and aunts. Fewer people will become grandparents. If parenthood itself is a developmental stage, important to full maturation of individual identity, fewer people will achieve this via their own children.

We think of ourselves as a society that loves children and, although most parents do, society as a whole does not. It is difficult for parents to care for, educate and enjoy their children when there is not support, or recognition, from the outside world. If present trends continue, one child in six will lose a parent through divorce before he/she is 18. We are one of the few nations with no family policy. Children need protection, nurturing and training for citizenship if they are to form healthy marriages in the future. Yet children are increasingly subject to either the stress of broken homes, or absent parents by reason of work. Children raised without strong meaningful family ties first show emotional and motivational symptoms: disaffection, indifference, irresponsibility and inability to follow through on activities requiring application and persistence. The end result is a young adult who is uninterested, disconnected and sometimes even hostile to people and activities in our society— including the institution of marriage.

Marriage presents some of the most difficult problems in human life. It begins by seeming to promise supreme happiness and demands in the end the most unselfish sacrifices from man and woman alike. Marriage can never be a matter of living happily ever after. Commitment requires ability. Natural aptitudes have to be trained.

There are many conflicting aspects of our society. Some of these can be interpreted in terms of deepening fragmentation, but the future quality of marriage and family life will depend, to a large extent, on what we can do with what we know. This book has addressed the problems of the individual couple in learning to stay with the pain of crisis, risking the death of old expectations but also witnessing the rebirth of a stronger relationship. Stronger marriages will strengthen the community but there also has to be work at the community level.

We have to see the family in relation to its social context — the world of work, of neighborhood and community. Day care programs, for example, could be developed to reach out into the home and community so that the entire neighborhood could be caught up in activities in behalf of its children. Opportunities have to be made for the part-time employment of mothers and for the enhancement of the status and power of women *in the home*. Children need to see adults in their work settings. They need to have jobs or carry real responsibilities with consequences they are held responsible for as they grow. The schools should prepare children for parenthood with courses on human development that would involve responsible active concern for the lives of young children and their families. Day care centers and preschool programs could be situated near the school so that the learning youngsters could work with the children on a regular basis and become acquainted with their families and the neighborhood. Much more could be done with urban planning and developing neighborhoods to allow children the liberty to be among people and things that excite them and fire their imagination. We need to design opportunities for children to be involved with both older people and younger children — settings where both old and young can just sit and talk.

The preparation for marriage is complex. The present

crisis that marriage is going through will undoubtedly result in many changes and has already done so. It needs this community concern for it involves not merely a sexual relationship between the couple but also tasks of managing a household in common, sharing parenthood and a great deal of economic cooperation. How these tasks are carried affects us all.

Appendix

Resources—A Personal Evaluation.

If you and your partner recognize that there are disruptive forces, behavior patterns or attitudes in your marriage, you may want help in developing a workable, productive marriage. No matter how hard you and your partner try, it is possible that your well established habits of thought and behavior patterns will negate your individual efforts. This appendix includes suggestions about readings and about types of therapists to assist you.

A word about reading: There are many excellent books on various aspects of marriage, some of which are listed below. The printed word can be picked up at any time. You as reader can pause and reflect, turn the pages back and the argument over, compare what is said with your own experience. You can appreciate the detail of evidence without being distracted by it. What is said comes usually from the context of experience of and with many couples. It does not define *you* but it can shed light on your situation and open up directions for action. What it cannot do is individualize your situation and address the particular nuances of your need. The *interactive* component and *your* contribution to it are difficult to see clearly by reading alone. Above all it is important not to use the book as a weapon, a way of labeling your partner. Readings are best used by you personally to widen your knowledge of options and to reflect on your own behavior.

Annotated Bibliography
for Your Further Reading:

Bach, George R., and Peter Wyden, *The Intimate Enemy: How To Fight Fair in Love and Marriage*. New York: William Morrow and Co. 1969.

This book is a self training program based in the idea that true intimacy can only thrive in healthy men and women if they fight. Fight-evaders who play "games" with their partners avoid also a deep emotional involvement with their partners and risk boredom, infidelity, misunderstanding and divorce. Dr. Bach is a clinical psychologist who trains people to "fight fair" and how to start and end a good fight.

Boxco, Antoinette, *Marriage Encounter: The Rediscovery of Love*. St. Meinrad, Indiana: Abbey Press, 1972.

This book examines the reasons why Marriage Encounter, a movement that combines psychology, religious values and experimental dialogue techniques for reviving the relationship between husband and wife, is meeting with such success. It looks into the history of the movement and also at some of the problems that have arisen and the possibilities for the future.

Comfort, Alex, *The Joy of Sex: A Gourmet Guide to Love Making*. New York: Simon and Schuster, 1972.

As an illustrated account of the full repetoire of human heterosexuality, this book has few peers. The author describes what to do about impotence or premature ejaculation, how to manage oral sex, how to play symbolically aggressive games, how to treat a partner who is hip for "discipline," how not to be bothered by fetishes and the use of kinky clothes as sex stimuli.

Francoeur, Robert T., *Eve's New Rib: Twenty Faces of Sex, Marriage and Family*. New York: Dell Publishing Co., 1972.

Francoeur examines the impact on contemporary and future patterns of marriage and family life of women's liberation, new reproductive technologies, contraceptive techniques and social aspects of the sexual revolution.

Ginott, Haim G., *Between Parent and Child: New Solutions to Old Problems*. New York: Avon Books, 1969.

Dr. Ginott's suggestions are direct and easily understood ways to establish a relationship of mutual responsibility, love and respect with your child.

Harding, Mary Esther, *The Way of All Women*. New York: C. G. Jung Foundation for Analytical Psychology, 1970.

This classic study of the psychological nature of woman was first published in 1933. It is a contemporary and timeless book.

Kempler, Walter, *Principles of Gestalt Family Therapy*. Privately printed in Norway by A.s Joh. Nordahls Trykkeri, Oslo, 1973.

This excellent small book is really for professional therapists but is an easily understood guide to effective marital communication and the identification of sources of misunderstanding.

Keyes, Margaret Frings, *The Inward Journey: Art as Therapy*. Millbrae, California: Celestial Arts, 1974.

Although this book focuses on the use of non-verbal art methods as means of understanding how you came to be the way you are and increasing your awareness of your direction of growth, there are many examples of couple interaction and their patterns of behavior. In the last section, the connections between Transactional Analysis, Gestalt Therapy and Jungian Depth Psychology, three of today's most popular systems of psychotherapy are described in easily understood terms and illustrated with examples from marriage relationships.

Lederer, William J., and Don D. Jackson, *The Mirages of Marriage*. New York: W. W. Norton, 1968.

Mr. Lederer's and Dr. Jackson's thesis is that marriage is a system in which the partners act and react to each other and to the total relationship in definable ways. Marriage cannot be dealt with by dealing with the partners as separate individuals. Dr. Don Jackson, a specialist in human communication and family relationships felt that the institution of marriage had failed to adapt itself sufficiently to current realities. "Plagued by guilt and uncertainty, (the partners) struggle to discover their identity yet are unable to *accept* themselves if they do catch a glimpse of their genuine needs, desires and goals. For what they glimpse is not what they have been conditioned to believe is "good" or "right" . . ." (p. 35)

Madow, Leo, *Anger: How to Recognize and Cope With It*. New York: Chas. Scribner's Sons, 1972.

This book shows how to recognize anger, some of the reasons for its development and what to do about it. One chapter deals with anger and sex.

Masters, William H., and Virginia E. Johnson in association with Robert J. Levin, *The Pleasure Bond: A New Look at Sexuality and Committment*. Boston: Little, Brown & Co., 1975.

This practical book addresses itself to the question of how a man and woman can keep alive the sexual excitement that originally united them. It posits that the most important communication takes place without words and equality of the sexes can heighten sexual responsiveness. It develops what loyalty and trust contribute to the sexual experience itself and how to resolve differences in physical desire. Some aspects of today's sexual revolution are proving destructive to intimate relationships and Masters and Johnson use their research evidence and clinical experience to illuminate the emotional elements that create the bond of pleasure as the ultimate source of personal commitment.

May, Rollo, *Love and Will*. New York: W. W. Norton and Co., Inc., 1969.

Dr. May analyzes the meanings of love and will, their sources and their interrelation. He explores *eros*, the daimonic and intentionality as aspects of relationship. This is a valuable book in understanding the value of the irrational in marriage.

Otto, Herbert, *More Joy in Your Marriage: Developing Your Marriage Potential*. New York: Cornerstone Library, 1969.

Dr. Otto is a clinical social worker concerned with the development of human potential in all aspects. In this book he gives a manual of methods and techniques to "wake up" marriage.

Powell, John, S.J., *Why Am I Afraid to Tell You Who I Am?* Chicago: Argus Communications.

This book offers insights on self awareness, personal growth and interpersonal communication. It is quite simplified and easily understood.

Rosenberg, Jack Lee, *Total Orgasm*. New York: Random House, 1973.

Orgasm is a natural body reflex action and given the right conditions it just happens. Because for many people, sexual union is barren of pleasure, this book offers breathing exercises and instruction in movements to build tension and energy in your body in a pattern that *simulates* the movements that automatically precede an orgasm. You learn how to tolerate more excitement and a more complete involvement with your partner.

Satir, Virginia, *Peoplemaking: Because You Want to be a Better Parent*. Palo Alto, California: Science and Behavior Books Inc., 1972.

Conjoint family therapy simplified for the layman, this book teaches basic communication skills and identifies problematic styles of family interaction.

Stevens, John O., *Awareness: Exploring, Experimenting, Experiencing*. Moab, Utah: Real People Press, 1971.

This book of awareness exercises has specific sections for couples and for married partners.

Ulanov, Ann Belford, *The Feminine: In Jungian Psychology and Christian Theology*. Evanston, Ill.: Northwestern University Press, 1971.

This book explores various aspects of the feminine as a style of consciousness not restricted to women alone but also an aspect of all men. The importance of developing a more inclusive consciousness is stressed for both sexes and some of the impoverishment in Western modes of thought as a result of the past suppression of the feminine.

Von Franz, Marie Louise, and James Hillman, *Jung's Typology*. New York: Spring Publications, 1971.

For those interested in learning more of the psychological types and the differences in how they perceive and form judgments, the first part of this book is particularly good.

Wickes, Frances G., *The Inner World of Choice*. New York: Harper and Row, 1963.

The author, a Jungian analyst, is concerned with the interior of the person, the pain of self knowledge, choice, responsibility, self awareness and self judgment. The stark necessity for confronting one's real inner life is the driving force of a book filled with fascinating case histories, sketches of dreams and concrete incidents. Four chapters— The Masculine Principle, The Woman in Man, The Feminine Principle, and The Man in Woman—are particularly valuable for understanding the Jungian view of the role of opposites in marriage, and the importance of their integration during the course of a lifetime.

The following journals have articles related to the themes explored in this book:

Psychology Today, PO Box 2990, Boulder, Colorado 80302
> This magazine presents in popular language current developments in psychology and research issues. It is usually well illustrated.

Synthesis, The Synthesis Press, 150 Doherty Way, Redwood City, California
> Unfortunately, there has only been one issue, Vol. 1, Number 1, 1974 but it contained superb articles on subpersonalities and the man-woman problem. Hopefully there will be more.

Psychological Perspectives, 10349 W. Pico Blvd., Los Angeles, California 90064
> This journal in its sixth year of publication has a Jungian point of view and a consistently high quality to the articles and book reviews.

Types of Marital Therapists

When you decide you need the skills of an objective third party, it is important to know something about the several classes of marital therapy and what these professionals can and cannot do for you. The following section describes the types of practitioners of marriage therapy, something of their training, and the areas of competence they claim and what they can and cannot do. How you might locate and assess the type of professional you choose has already been described in chapter seven.

Your personal assessment that this is a person you and your partner can work with is essential. If you do not feel this trust, contact someone else.

The Clinical Social Worker

Most social workers have earned their M.S.W. (Master of Social Work) degree by completion of a rigorous two year program of graduate study in an accredited school of social work. This follows 4 years of college with a major in behavioral science. In addition to the required academic study, social work students work two or three days each week in an agency which offers counseling services, such as a psychiatric clinic, a hospital, or a family counseling agency. This on-the-job training is carefully supervised by an experienced social worker. Social workers do marriage counseling and family therapy in community agencies and increasingly in private practice. Licensed clinical social workers have had a minimum of 5 years postgraduate experience in agencies. They are licensed psychotherapists as well as marriage and family counselors and such experienced workers have traditionally formed the staff for family service agencies. As noted in the previous chapter, there are various theoretical orientations in the practice of psychotherapy and it is important to you to inquire as to the social worker's training and method. Social workers more than any other group have been trained to take into account the social and community context of their clients' psychological problems. They deal with the practical realities of money and health problems as well as the psychological defenses which interfere with communication between partners. There has been confusion in public knowledge of the clinical social worker's skills because public welfare workers without graduate training are also called social workers. They are not professional counselors.

The Clinical Psychologist

The clinical psychologist has a Ph.D. degree usually obtained with 4 years of postgraduate study and training. To qualify as a clinical (i.e. someone who may treat patients) psychologist he/she must have had the majority of his/her training in clinical work rather than experimental, educational, social or general psychology. Because the psychologist does not have the M.D. degree he is not allowed to administer drugs or other forms of physical treatment — insulin or electric shock. Some universities offer an M.S. in psychology and give minimal training in counseling and testing in this year of graduate study. Recently programs in humanistic psychology have begun to offer more clinical training at the master's degree level. Before consulting a psychologist who does not have his Ph.D. the prospective patient should be especially careful to check the nature of his training.

The Psychiatrist

Although in recent years, psychiatrists have become more interested in the family and in marriage, their training generally does not prepare them to deal with marital problems in terms of the marital interaction. The ordinary psychiatrist spends 4 years in medical school, one year in a general internship and at least 3 years in psychiatric residency. A good part of his/her residency may have been at a large mental institution or state hospital and the people he/she dealt with as patients were hospitalized for severe mental illnesses like schizophrenia or alcoholism. He/she spent a half year or so working with neurological problems and some time in an outpatient clinic seeing adults and perhaps also children, usually in individual therapy once or twice a week. More institutions are beginning to offer special training in family and marital work and have opened family treatment units but this has not been common. Psychoanalysts, often the best trained psychiatrists in their area (with additional psychoanalytic training after their three years of psychiatric residency) are handicapped in handling marital problems by their tradition that one spouse is seen by one therapist and the other by another therapist. The two analysts rarely, if ever, communicate, so important data about the marital interaction, as such, does not surface.

When the psychiatrist has developed family and marital treatment skills as well as medical skills, however, his/her presence in a cotherapy team is invaluable. Some problematic behaviors and feelings have a physiological basis. Sometimes medication, particularly for overwhelming depression, is useful as an adjunct to what is being accomplished in the interpersonal treatment relationship. The psychiatrist's methods of practice can be ascertained by asking someone about them who has seen him/her in therapy or sometimes in a brief telephone conversation directly with the psychiatrist. If at all possible, partners who have agreed to seek marital therapy should interview the prospective therapists together. This may seem expensive but the investment is crucial.

The Pastoral Counselor and the Marriage Counselor

The pastoral counseling group is a rather specialized branch of the ministry. Some members have a D.D. (Doctor of Divinity) degree and some have taken additional courses in educational psychology, clinical psychology or pastoral counseling. However the well trained pastoral counselor is still rare. This is not to say that consulting with one's priest or minister cannot be a quite valuable step to take. Sometimes what the minister lacks in formal training, he has in practical experience of human nature. Often the relief of simply talking out that which has been kept inside is enough to gain necessary perspective to continue.

The average nonpastoral marriage counselor has an MA degree in the field of psychology, educational psychology, counseling and testing or religion. In California and some other states licensing is required before one can advertise in the telephone directories as a marriage counselor. Graduate study emphasizing marriage and family and supervised experience is becoming mandatory for new practitioners. Professional associations are pushing for further training qualifications. Marriage counselors are *not* licensed to practice psychotherapy.

Community Agencies

As noted before, you can locate private practice marriage counselors through the professional associations of the type of professional — doctor, social worker, psychologist, counselor — you prefer. There also are Family Service Agencies, Catholic Social Service, Jewish Family Service Agency and the Salvation Army Agencies which employ professionals and through Community funding can offer help according to a fee scale based on your income rather than the actual cost of the services. Although the workers may not always be as highly experienced as those in private practice, they have a system of staff supervision and ongoing training which guarantees a high quality of service. It often means that many options for treatment are available, for instance, work in group as well as individual therapy and family group therapy. Often more than one staff member is involved with the family. Services for children may include psychological testing as well as play therapy. The services of a team of consultants are available to staff members in assessing the family needs and the needs of the marital relationship. Such a range of services is more likely to be found in larger metropolitan centers than elsewhere but the network of good family agencies is extensive.

Nonprofessionals

Another resource to be considered is the family member whose advice you value or the close friend. Often unburdening yourself is helpful and the other person can offer his/her experience and practical advice. You know he/she sees you and cares about you. This however can also be a difficulty in that you may not be seen objectively. Usually friends are not equally involved with both partners. They also tend not to challenge and to push you to examine your own involvement in the difficulty too deeply. They may lack experience in the particular facets that are troubling you and not know how to get the relevant facts in focus. There are other considerations, primarily the privacy of the marital relationship. Professional service involves confidentiality. Sometimes in a time of hurt or anger, you may present a picture of your partner that seems to your friend who does not see the whole picture, intolerable. You may then be affirmed in a position which you do not want to hold in the long run and find it difficult to back away from the "stand" you have taken.

Resources in Group Movements

A phenomenon of our times is the growing number of large group movements which are concerned with increasing consciousness in the individual and his/her ability to cope with and find meaning in life. The encounter group movement was the forerunner. The emphasis was on authenticity in personal relationships and straight messages concerning one's feelings. "Openness" was advocated and "risking" testing one's assumptions concerning oneself and other people. There was new excitement in owning attributes one had rather discredited before. For some people, the harder "attack therapy" tactics of Synanon seemed necessary to them to puncture their own defenses and bring about changed behavior. The "games" (Synanon sessions) with couples encouraged wild engrossment of charge and counter charge to the ultimate absurdity so that painful insight into · one's own role could come along with healing laughter. EST (Erhart Seminar Training) is a movement more characteristic of the 70's. Lectures are offered which distill insights from various psychological systems and eastern philosophies together with experiential exercises and then large group sharing of what it all meant. Its powerful impact is attested in the large number of volunteers who give their time to this commercial business operation. The foregoing, although they deal with marriages and nonmarried couple relationships, do not focus on them directly and always emphasize the primacy of the individual's self interest.

Other large group movements do focus on the couple relationship as such. Marriage Encounter in this country is a variant of a movement in Spain. It takes the primacy of the marriage commitment for granted and then deals with the reality that most marriages function with very little spark or vitality. A weekend is spent with approximately 20 other couples and three laymen leading couples who share from their written journals. The couple spends much of their time alone, writing their reflections on various core questions. They then share their written reflections with each other and dialogue in closely timed segments. They do not open their experiences to the larger group but increasingly they are trained in sharing their deepest feelings with their partner. For many it is the first time this level of intimacy has been reached. For some it is the first time they have really known their own thought-feeling. Although not restricted to Roman Catholics, the movement is presently drawing its clientele from church related people. (For further information contact Barbara and Armando Carlo, Marriage Encounter, 5305 W. Foster Ave., Chicago, Ill. 60630.)

The Creative Initiative Foundation is another nonprofit group led by nonprofessionals in the sense of therapists or church leaders but they too have a strong values orientation which has a religious flavor. They have developed an interesting blend of experiential group methods to examine structure, function, and need in marriage as the "givens" which already exist and with which each couple must come to terms and accept. They emphasize a dialogue method, a process of conscious interaction between the individual and the "givens." This results in specific outcomes for the individual, which in turn carries implications for the community of "one world." (Creative Initiative Foundation, 2555 Park Blvd., Suite #20, Palo Alto, California 94306.)

ACME the Association of Couples for Marriage Enrichment, a new national organization for married couples has its headquarters in North Carolina (403 South Hawthorne Road, Winston-Salem, N.C. 27103) but has member couples in all 50 states. Their purpose is to support couples in enriching their own marriages. They promote effective community services to foster successful marriages and know the resources in each community to make referrals to counselors, to books on marriage, programs, growth groups and marriage enrichment retreats. Well Being is a national organization founded by Frank and Barbara Potter, 101 Ross Ave., San Anselmo, California 94960 with a similar purpose but emphasis is the family in a community of families to make up for the loss of the extended family. They provide resource material on building such communities. A recent and very promising development is that of family clusters with 27 to 28 people from 4 or more families who meet together regularly and are involved on many levels between the generations of different families. Dena Nye and Trevor Hoy of the Berkeley Center for Human Interaction, 1816 Scenic Ave., Berkeley are developing a training program on how to get these clusters started and leadership in them.

Index

Adult development, 95-99
Affection, need for, 101-102
  exercises, 103
    see also Sex and affection
Al-Anon, 68, 74
Al-Ateen, 68, 74
Alcohol, 50, 64-68
  exercises concerning, 73-74
Alcoholics Anonymous, 68, 74
Anger, expression, 4-6, 79-82
  among women, 57
Aristotle, 133
Association of Couples for Marriage
    Enrichment (ACME), 155

Belonging, need for, 101
  exercises, 103
Berne, Eric, 11
Bodily sensations and feelings, 77
Body language, 75-76

Children, behavior and marital crisis,
    32-33
  discipline of, 115
  exercises concerning, 72-73
  and marital therapy, 50, 63-64
  training for marriage, 138-140
Clinical psychologist, 151
Clinical social worker, 150-151
Commitment, 58-61
Communication, process, 79
  and reconnecting, 75-82
  and self-worth, 57
  techniques, 50
    see also Exercises
Community agencies and marriage
    counseling, 152-153
Community, and marriage, 139
Companionship, and marriage, 134
Conflict, and anger, 5-6
  resolution of, 91-93
Confrontation, 135
Conjoint family therapy, 110
Consciousness, growth of, 94, 134
Control, exercises, 103
  need for, 101
    see also Power and control
Creative Initiative Foundation, 155
Crisis, case history, 116-119
  growth and, 1-3, 8, 114
  and renegotiation, 23-28
Death, 99
Demands, 10

Depth Psychology, 12
Divorce, 113-114

EST (Erhart Seminar Training), 154
Exercises, alcoholism, 73-74
  art, 131-132
  belonging, 103
  children, 72-75
  conflict resolution, 91-93
  family sculpture, 33-38
  feelings, 8-10, 76-82
  Inward Journey case history, 123-131
  marriage strengths, 103-106
  money, 68-69
  past experiences, 47-49
  power, 69-70, 103
  sex and affection, 70-72, 103
  subpersonalities, 28-29
  tape recording of voice, 76
Extramarital affairs, 58
Extroverts, 83-85

Family, messages, 37-39
  patterns and change, 134-140
  sculpture, 30, 33-38
    see also Conjoint therapy
Family Service Association, 110
Fear and sexuality, 59-60
Feelings, cover, 4
  exercises with, 8-10
  expression of, 7-10, 76-82
Feminine function, 54-57
  and marriage, 136
Fighting, 117, 119-120
Finances, planning, 53
  responsibility, 52
    see also Money

Gestalt Psychology, 12
  impasse phase, 19
  and marriage therapy, 110
  and subpersonalities, 22
Gould, Roger, 95
Gray Power, 99
Grievances, 78
Group movements, 153-155
Guilt, 4-5

"Haircut" technique, 81-82
Hidden personalities,
    see Subpersonalities
Homosexuality, 136-138

Intensive individual treatment, 123-131
Introvert type, 83-85
Intuition, 83-85, 89
Inward Journey, 123-131

Judging ability, 83
Jung, Carl, 12, 83
Jungian analysis, 110

Kempler, Walter, 119

Lamers, William M., 7
Listening effectively, 75-82
"Living together," 135-136

Malinowski, Bronislaw, 136
Marriage, and adult development,
    95-99
  alternatives to, 134-138
  goals, 95
  and personal needs, 100-102
  preparation for, 138-140
  resources in, 89-90
  strengths, 103-106
  therapy types, 149-155
Marriage contract, 111-113
Marriage counselor, 151-152
Marriage Encounter, 7, 154
Marriage therapy, 107-111, 114-116,
    149-155
Masculine function, 54-55
  and marriage, 136
Men's Liberation, 136
Money, 50-53
  and adult development, 96-99
  exercises, 68-69

Needs, personal, 61-62, 100-102, 112
Neurosis, 43
Nonprofessional marriage counseling,
    153

Open marriage, 56, 135
Otto, Herbert, 104

Parent Effectiveness Training
    (P.E.T.), 64
Pastoral counselors, 151-152
Perception, 83-85, 89
Perls, Fritz, 12
Personality, 82-89
Power and control, 50, 54-57
  and children, 63-64
  exercises, 69-70

and sex roles, 56-57
Professional help, 3-4
    see also Marriage therapy
Psychiatry, 149-150
Psychoanalytic therapy, 110

Questioning techniques, 78-79

Readings, usefulness of, 141
Renegotiation, 113-114
Resentment, 79
Risk-taking, 91, 135
Roles, current definitions, 39-40
  work, 28, 54-55
    See also Feminine function,
    Masculine function,
    Subpersonalities

Security, 52
    see also Money
Self-acceptance, sexual, 58
Self-formation, 95, 98
Self-perception, 6
Self-rejection, 43
Sex and affection, 50, 57-63
  exercises, 70-72
Sexual bond, 59
Sexual intercourse, conflicts, 62-63
  exercises with, 71-72
Society for Clinical Social Work, 110
Struggle, 119-120
    see also Fighting
Subpersonalities, 12-29, 30-32
  acceptance of, 21-29
  defined, 16
  dominant, 18, 110
  exercises with, 28-29
  integration of, 18-20, 40
  and marriage partnership, 20-29,
    113
Subself, *see* Subpersonalities
Synanon, 154

Thinking type, 83, 89
Transactional Analysis, 11-12
  and alcoholism 64-66
  ego states, 42-46
  and marriage therapy, 110

Values, 6, 50
"Vesuvius" technique, 80-81

Wall of Trivia, 45-46
Women's Liberation, 54, 134
Work roles, 28, 54-55

Margaret Frings Keyes, M.S.W., author of *The Inward Journey,* is a psychotherapist in private practice in San Francisco who has had intensive and extensive experience working with individuals, with couples, with families, and with groups. She has taught marriage therapy and also the use of art methods in psychotherapy. She trained as a Transactional Analyst with Eric Berne and as a Gestalt therapist with Fritz Perls.